iPad®

FOR DUMMIES®

POCKET EDITION

by Edward C. Baig
USA TODAY Personal Tech columnist
and
Bob LeVitus
Houston Chronicle "Dr. Mac"
columnist

WILEY

John Wiley & Sons, Inc.

iPad® For Dummies®, Pocket Edition

Published by
John Wiley & Sons, Inc.
111 River Street
Hoboken, NJ 07030-5774
www.wiley.com

Copyright © 2011 by John Wiley & Sons, Inc., Hoboken, New Jersey

Published by John Wiley & Sons, Inc., Hoboken, New Jersey

Published simultaneously in Canada

For general information on our products and services, please contact our Customer Care Department within the U.S. at 877-762-2974, outside the U.S. at 317-572-3993, or fax 317-572-4002.

For technical support, please visit www.wiley.com/techsupport.

Wiley publishes in a variety of print and electronic formats and by print-on-demand. Some material included with standard print versions of this book may not be included in e-books or in print-on-demand. If this book refers to media such as a CD or DVD that is not included in the version you purchased, you may download this material at http://booksupport.wiley.com. For more information about Wiley products, visit www.wiley.com

ISBN 978-1-118-08400-7 (pbk); ISBN 978-1-118-11872-6 (ebk)

Manufactured in the United States of America

10 9 8 7 6 5 4 3 2

WILEY

Publisher's Acknowledgments

We're proud of this book; please send us your comments through our online registration form located at www.dummies.com/register/.

Some of the people who helped bring this book to market include the following:

Acquisitions and Editorial

Project Editor: Jodi Jensen

Executive Editor: Bob Woerner

Special Help: Brian Walls, Thomas Miller

Composition Services

Project Coordinator: Kristie Rees

Layout and Graphics: Samantha K. Cherolis, Joyce Haughey, SDJumper

Proofreader: The Well-Chosen Word, Susan Moritz

Publishing and Editorial for Technology Dummies

Richard Swadley, Vice President and Executive Group Publisher

Andy Cummings, Vice President and Publisher

Mary Bednarek, Executive Acquisitions Director

Mary C. Corder, Editorial Director

Publishing for Consumer Dummies

Kathleen Nebenhaus, Vice President and Executive Publisher

Composition Services

Debbie Stailey, Director of Composition Services

Table of Contents

Introduction..1

About This Book...1

Icons Used in This Book....................................2

Chapter 1: Getting to Know Your iPad.................3

Turning the iPad On and Off................................4

Locking the iPad...4

Exploring the iPad's Big Picture..........................5

The iPad as an iPod......................................5

The iPad as an Internet communications device........6

The iPad as an e-book reader.........................6

The iPad and third-party apps.......................7

What do you need to use your iPad?................7

Touring the iPad's Exterior...............................8

On the top edge...8

On the bottom edge......................................9

On the sides, front and back.........................10

Status bar..13

The iPad's Stupendous Home Screen Icons............15

Chapter 2: Mastering Multitouch.....................19

Training Your Digits...20

Navigating beyond Home....................................20

The Incredible Virtual Keyboard.........................22

Discovering the special-use keys..................24

Finger-typing on the virtual keyboards...........25

Editing mistakes..28

Select, cut, copy, and paste.........................29

Multitasking...31

Organizing Icons into Folders.............................33

Printing..35

Searching for Content......................................36

Chapter 3: Getting Stuff to and from Your iPad......37

Starting to Sync..38

Disconnecting the iPad.....................................43

Synchronizing Your Data....................................44

iCloud...44

Contacts..44

Calendars 46
Mail accounts..47
Other..48
Synchronizing Your Media...48
Apps 49
Ringtones 51
Music, music videos, and voice memos....................51
Movies 52
TV shows 53
Podcasts...54
iTunes U 55
Books 56
Photos...57
Using the Notification Center 58

Chapter 4: Surfing and Sending: Web and Messaging. . .61

Surfin' Dude..61
Exploring the browser...62
Blasting off into cyberspace......................................63
I Can See Clearly Now 65
Using the Reading List...67
Putting Reminders to Work...68
Setting Up Your E-Mail..69
Set up your account the easy way 70
Set up your account the less easy way 70
Darling, You Send Me..71
Sending an all-text message.......................................71
Sending a photo with a text message 74
Replying to or forwarding an e-mail message 74
Working with Mail Messages 76
Reading messages 76
Managing messages 77
Doing the iMessage Thing..78

Chapter 5: Music, Movies, and Books 81

Introducing the iPod inside Your iPad 82
Playing with the Audio Controls 84
Using the Genius feature...88
Creating playlists 89
Finding Stuff to Watch 90
Playing Video 93
Chatting with a View: FaceTime 95
Shooting Photos and Video..96
Shopping for E-Books...97

Browsing the iBookstore....................................98
Searching the iBookstore..................................99
Buying a book from the iBookstore..............................100
Buying books beyond Apple..............................100
Finding free books outside the iBookstore..............101
Reading a Book..102
Turn pages...102
Jump to a specific page............................104
Go to table of contents............................104
Add bookmarks.......................................105
Change the type size and font..................106
Search inside and outside a book..............106
Perusing with Newsstand..............................107

Chapter 6: Gotta Love Those Apps! 109

Tapping the Magic of Apps..............................109
Using Your Computer to Find Apps..................111
Browsing the App Store from your computer..........112
Using the Search field..............................114
Getting more information about an app..........115
Downloading an app................................116
Using Your iPad to Find Apps..........................117
Browsing the App Store on your iPad..........117
Using the Search field..............................119
Finding details about an app......................119
Downloading an app................................121
Updating and re-downloading an app..........121
Working with Apps..122
Deleting an app.......................................123
Socializing with Social Media Apps..................124
Game Center...125
Facebook..127
MySpace...128
Twitter...128

Chapter 7: Ten Worthwhile Accessories 131

Casing the iPad...132
Protecting the Screen....................................133
Exploring Physical Keyboards..........................133
Connecting a Camera.....................................134
Connecting to a TV or Projector......................134
Keeping a Spare Charger................................135
Listening the Wired and Bluetooth Ways..........135
Listening with Speakers..................................136
Docking with an Extender Cable......................136
Keeping Your iPad Upright..............................137

Introduction

● ●

As Yogi Berra would say, "It was déjà vu all over again": Front-page treatment, top billing on network TV and cable, and diehards lining up days in advance to ensure landing a highly lusted-after product from Apple. Like its revolutionary predecessors, the iPhone and the iPod, the iPad is now hot indeed. But we trust you didn't pick up this book to read yet another account about how the iPad launch was an epochal event. We trust you *did* buy the book to find out how to get the very most out of your remarkable device — especially the new features provided in Apple's iOS 5 update. Whether you have an iPad or the new iPad 2, our goal is to deliver that information in a light and breezy fashion.

About This Book

We think you're pretty darn smart for buying a *For Dummies* book. That says to us that you have the confidence and intelligence to know what you don't know. As with most Apple products, however, the iPad is beautifully designed and intuitive to use. You'll get pretty far just by exploring the iPad's many functions and features on your own, without the help of this (or any other) book. However, this book is chockfull of useful tips, advice, and other nuggets that should make your iPad experience all the more pleasurable.

Icons Used in This Book

Little round pictures (icons) appear in the left margins throughout this book. Consider these icons miniature road signs, telling you something extra about the topic at hand or hammering a point home.

Here's what the four icons used in this book look like and mean.

 These are the juicy morsels, shortcuts, and recommendations that might make the task at hand faster or easier.

 This icon emphasizes the stuff we think you ought to retain. You may even jot down a note to yourself in the iPad.

 Put on your propeller beanie hat and pocket protector; this text includes the truly geeky stuff. You can safely ignore this material, but if it weren't interesting or informative, we wouldn't have bothered to write it.

 You wouldn't intentionally run a stop sign, would you? In the same fashion, ignoring warnings may be hazardous to your iPad and (by extension) your wallet. There, you now know how these warning icons work, for you have just received your very first warning!

Chapter 1

Getting to Know Your iPad

In This Chapter

▶ Turning the device on and off and locking it

▶ Looking at the big picture

▶ Touring the outside of the iPad 2

▶ Discovering the stupendous Home screen

Congratulations! You've selected one of the most incredible handheld devices we've ever seen. The iPad 2 is a combination of a killer audio and video iPod, an e-book reader, a powerful Internet communications device, a movie and still camera, a video chat terminal, a superb handheld gaming device, and a platform for over 300,000 apps at the time this was written.

In this chapter, we offer a gentle introduction to all the pieces that make up your iPad, plus overviews of its revolutionary hardware and software features.

Turning the iPad On and Off

Apple has taken the time to partially charge your iPad 2, so you get some measure of instant gratification. After taking it out of the box, press and hold the Sleep/Wake button on the upper-right edge. At first, you see the famous Apple logo, followed a few seconds later by a connection symbol (the USB cable leading to an iTunes icon). This is your cue to sync your iPad 2, which we cover later, in Chapter 3.

To turn the device completely off, press and hold the Sleep/Wake button again until a red arrow appears at the top of the screen. Then drag the arrow from the left to the right with your finger. Tap Cancel at the bottom of the screen if you change your mind.

Locking the iPad

Here are some sound reasons for locking your iPad:

- ✔ You can't inadvertently turn it on.
- ✔ You keep prying eyes at bay.
- ✔ You spare the battery some juice.

Apple makes it a cinch to lock the iPad.

In fact, you don't need to do anything to lock the iPad; by default, it happens automatically as long as you don't touch the screen for a minute or two. You can change this delay time from the General pane of the Settings screen.

Can't wait? To lock the iPad immediately, press the Sleep/Wake button.

Unlocking the iPad is easy, too. Here's how it works:

1. **Press the Sleep/Wake button. Or, press the Home button on the front of the screen.**

   Either way, the on-screen slider appears.

2. **Drag the slider to the right with your finger.**

3. **In some cases, you also need to enter a passcode.**

Exploring the iPad's Big Picture

The iPad has many best-of-class features, but perhaps its most unusual feature is the lack of a physical keyboard or stylus. Instead, it has a 9.7-inch super-high-resolution touchscreen (132 pixels per inch at 1024 x 748 resolution, if you care about such things) that you operate with your finger.

Another feature that knocked our socks off was the iPad's built-in sensors. An accelerometer detects when you rotate the device from portrait to landscape mode and instantly adjusts what's on the display accordingly.

The following sections take a brief look at some of the iPad's features, broken down by product category.

The iPad as an iPod

The iPad is magical — and without a doubt, the best iPod Apple has ever produced. You can enjoy all your existing iPod content on the iPad's gorgeous high-resolution color display, which is bigger, brighter, and richer than any iPod or iPhone display that came before it.

 Bottom line: If you can get the content — be it video, audio, or whatever — into iTunes on your Mac or PC, you can synchronize (sync) it and watch or listen to it on your iPad. You can read more about syncing in Chapter 3.

If you get an error message about an incompatible video file, select the file in iTunes on your computer and choose Advanced⇨Create iPad or AppleTV Version. When the conversion is finished, sync again.

The iPad as an Internet communications device

Not only is the iPad a stellar iPod, but it's also a full-featured Internet communications device with a rich HTML e-mail client that's compatible with most POP and IMAP mail services, with support for Microsoft Exchange ActiveSync. Also on-board is a world-class Web browser (Safari) that, unlike on many mobile devices, makes Web surfing fun and easy on the eyes. Chapter 4 explains how to surf the Web using Safari.

You'll also find details about iMessage, the new 3G/Wi-Fi messaging app, in Chapter 4 — send unlimited photos, videos and contacts as well as text to any iOS 5 device. Plus, you can assign groups to easily keep all of your friends up-to-date. iOS 5 even integrates Twitter into many of your favorite apps, including Safari, Camera, Maps, and YouTube!

There's been a lot of buzz about the iPad 2's built-in FaceTime application, and no wonder — it allows you to chat with another FaceTime user over a Wi-Fi Internet connection, complete with audio and real-time video! We cover FaceTime in Chapter 5.

The iPad as an e-book reader

Download the free iBooks app from the App Store, and you'll discover a whole new way of finding and reading books. The iBookstore, covered in Chapter 5, is chock full of good reading at prices that are lower than a hardcover copy. And best of all, a great number of books are absolutely free.

iOS 5 also introduces Newsstand, the central storage spot for all of your magazine and newspaper application subscriptions.

The iPad and third-party apps

Over 300,000 iPhone apps are available at this writing, in categories that include games, business, education, entertainment, healthcare and fitness, music, photography, productivity, travel, sports, and many more. Most of those iPhone apps run flawlessly on the iPad. Meanwhile, at the time we wrote this, the App Store offered over 50,000 apps designed specifically for the iPad's large screen, with many more on the way. Chapter 6 helps you fill your iPad with all the cool apps your heart desires.

What do you need to use your iPad?

To actually *use* your iPad, only a few simple things are required. Here is a list of everything you need:

- ✔ An original iPad or iPad 2 (running iOS 5, if you want to take advantage of all the new features covered in this book)
- ✔ An iTunes Store account (assuming you want to acquire apps, videos, music, iBooks, podcasts, and the like, which you almost certainly do)
- ✔ Internet access — broadband wireless Internet access recommended

Plus you need *one* of the following:

- ✔ A Mac with a USB 2.0 port, Mac OS X Lion version 10.7 or later, and iTunes 10.4.1 or later
- ✔ A PC with a USB 2.0 port; Windows 7, Windows Vista, or Windows XP Home or Professional with Service Pack 3 or later; and iTunes 10.2 or later

Touring the iPad's Exterior

The iPad is a harmonious combination of hardware and software. The following sections look at the hardware — what's on the outside.

On the top edge

On the top of your iPad, you'll find the headphone jack, and the Sleep/Wake button, as shown in Figure 1-1:

✔ **On/Off, Sleep/Wake button:** This button is used to put your iPad's screen to sleep or to wake it up. It's also how you turn your iPad on or off. To put it to sleep or wake it up, just press the button. To turn it on or off, press and hold the button for a few seconds.

When your iPad is sleeping, nothing happens if you touch its screen. To wake it up, merely press the button again or press the Home button on the front of the device (as described in a moment).

✔ **Headphone jack:** This jack lets you plug in a headset. You can use headphones that came with your iPhone or iPod or any headphones or headset that plugs into a 3.5-mm stereo headphone jack.

✔ **Microphone:** This tiny dot has moved from next to the headphone jack on the original iPad to the center of the top edge on the iPad 2. It's actually a pretty good microphone.

Your iPad doesn't include the Voice Notes app that comes with the iPhone, but the App Store offers several free voice-recording apps for the iPad.

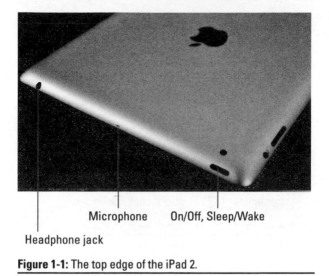

Microphone   On/Off, Sleep/Wake

Headphone jack

Figure 1-1: The top edge of the iPad 2.

On the bottom edge

On the bottom of your iPad are the speaker and dock connector, as shown in Figure 1-2:

- **Speaker:** The speaker plays audio if no headset is plugged in.

- **30-pin dock connector:** This connector has two purposes. One, you can use it to recharge your iPad's battery: Simply connect one end of the included dock connector–to–USB cable to the dock connector and the other end to the USB power adapter. Two, you can use the dock connector to synchronize your iPad with your computer: Connect one end of the same cable to the dock connector and the other end to a USB port on your Mac or PC.

Speaker   30-pin dock connector

Figure 1-2: The bottom edge of the iPad 2.

On the sides, front and back

Here's what you'll find on the right edge of your iPad (see Figure 1-3):

✔ **Side switch:** With the iPad 2, you can set this switch as either a silent (mute) switch or a screen rotation lock from within the Settings app. When configured as a silent switch and set to silent mode — the down position, with an orange dot visible on the switch — your iPad doesn't make any sound when you receive new mail or an alert pops up on the screen. However, it doesn't silence iTunes or Videos apps, nor will it mute games and other apps that include noises. When set as a screen rotation lock, it prevents your screen orientation from changing when you rotate your iPad.

To change the function of the side switch, tap the Settings icon on the Home screen and choose General⇨Use Side Switch To Mute or Use Side Switch to Lock Rotation.

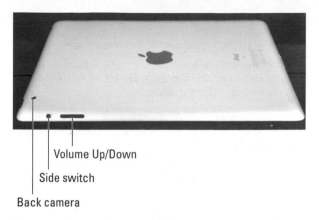

Volume Up/Down

Side switch

Back camera

Figure 1-3: Right side view of the iPad 2.

✔ **Volume Up/Down control:** This control is a single button that's just below the screen rotation lock. The upper part of the button increases the volume; the lower part decreases it.

If you're using an iPad with 3G hardware, you may see a Micro-SIM card tray on the left side of the device. This tray is used to install a Micro-SIM card from your cellular provider.

On the front of your iPad, you find the following (labeled in Figure 1-4):

✔ **Front Camera:** Your iPad 2 sports not one but two camera lenses — this one faces forward, allowing two-way video chatting in FaceTime. (More about FaceTime in Chapter 5.)

✔ **Touchscreen:** You find out how to use the iPad's gorgeous high-resolution color touchscreen in Chapter 2.

✔ **Home button:** No matter what you're doing, you can press the Home button at any time to display the Home screen, as shown in Figure 1-4.

✔ **Application buttons:** Each of the buttons (icons) shown on the screen in Figure 1-4 launches an included iPad application.

On the back of your iPad 2, in the top-left corner, you'll find another camera lens for taking video and still photos.

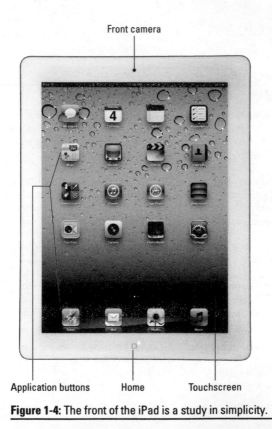

Front camera

Application buttons   Home   Touchscreen

Figure 1-4: The front of the iPad is a study in simplicity.

Status bar

The status bar, which is at the top of the screen, displays tiny icons that provide a variety of information about the current state of your iPad:

Airplane mode (Wi-Fi + 3G models only): You're allowed to use your iPod on a plane after the captain gives the word. But you can't use a cell phone or iPad Wi-Fi + 3G except when the plane is in the gate area before takeoff or after landing. Fortunately, your iPad offers an airplane mode, which turns off all wireless features of your iPad — the cellular, 3G, GPRS (General Packet Radio Service), and EDGE networks; Wi-Fi; and Bluetooth — and makes it possible to enjoy music or video during your flight.

3G (Wi-Fi + 3G models only): This icon informs you that the high-speed 3G data network from your wireless carrier (that's AT&T or Verizon in the United States) is available and that your iPad can connect to the Internet via 3G.

GPRS (Wi-Fi + 3G models only): This icon says that your wireless carrier's GPRS data network is available and that your iPad can use it to connect to the Internet.

EDGE (Wi-Fi + 3G models only): This icon tells you that your wireless carrier's EDGE network is available and you can use it to connect to the Internet.

Wi-Fi: If you see the Wi-Fi icon, it means your iPad is connected to the Internet over a Wi-Fi network. The more semicircular lines you see (up to three), the stronger the Wi-Fi signal. If you have only one or two semicircles of Wi-Fi strength, try moving around a bit. If you don't see the Wi-Fi icon in the status bar, Internet access is not currently available.

 Activity: This icon tells you that some network or other activity is occurring, such as over-the-air synchronization, sending or receiving e-mail, or loading a Web page.

 VPN: This icon shows that you are currently connected to a virtual private network (VPN).

 Lock: This icon tells you when your iPad is locked, as I mentioned earlier in this chapter.

 Play: This icon informs you that a song is currently playing.

Bluetooth: This icon indicates the current state of your iPad's Bluetooth connection. If you see this icon in the status bar, Bluetooth is on and a device (such as a wireless headset or keyboard) is connected. If the icon is gray (as shown on the right in the picture in the margin), Bluetooth is turned on but no device is connected. If the icon is white (as shown on the left in the picture in the margin) Bluetooth is on and one or more devices is connected. If you don't see a Bluetooth icon at all, Bluetooth is turned off.

 Screen rotation lock: This icon appears when the Screen Rotation Lock is engaged.

Battery: This icon reflects the level of your battery's charge. It's completely filled when you are not connected to a power source and your battery is fully charged (as shown in the margin). It then empties as your battery becomes depleted. The icon shows when you're connected to a power source and when the battery is now fully charged or is currently charging. You see an onscreen message when the charge drops to 20% or below and another when it reaches 10%.

The iPad's Stupendous Home Screen Icons

The Home screen offers 20 icons by default, each representing a different built-in application or function.

To get to your Home screen, tap the Home button (refer to Figure 1-4). If your iPad is asleep when you tap, the unlock screen appears. After it is unlocked, you see whichever page of icons was on the screen when it went to sleep.

Three steps let you rearrange icons on your iPad:

1. **Press and hold any icon until all the icons begin to "wiggle."**

2. **Drag the icons around until you're happy with their positions.**

3. **Press the Home button to save your arrangement and stop the "wiggling."**

If you haven't rearranged your icons, you see the following applications on your Home screen, starting at the top left:

 ✔ **Messages:** Send and receive unlimited messages with any iOS 5 device, including the iPhone and iPod touch. Your messages can include photos, video, contacts and current locations. Chapter 4 explains more about iMessage.

 ✔ **Calendar:** If you use iCal, Microsoft Entourage, or Microsoft Outlook as your calendar program on your PC or Mac, you can synchronize events between your computer, other iOS devices, and your iPad. Create an event on one device, and the event is automatically synchronized with the other device via iCloud.

✔ **Notes:** This program enables you to type notes when you're out and about. You can send the notes to yourself or to anyone else through e-mail, or save them on your iPad until you need them.

✔ **Reminders:** This new app makes it easy to organize your time by setting to-do lists, complete with reminders that are automatically updated across all your devices and Mac computers. Reminders can even be triggered by your arrival at a specific location.

✔ **Maps:** This app lets you view street maps or satellite imagery of locations around the globe, or ask for directions, traffic conditions, or even the location of a nearby pizza joint.

✔ **YouTube:** This app lets you watch videos from the popular YouTube Web site.

✔ **Videos:** This app is the repository for your movies, TV shows, and music videos. You add videos via iTunes on your Mac or PC, through iCloud or by purchasing them from the iTunes Store using the iTunes app on your iPad.

✔ **Contacts:** Like the Calendar app, this app synchronizes with the iCal, Entourage, or Outlook on your Mac or PC. You can synchronize contacts between your computer and your iPad. If you create a contact on one device, the contact is automatically synchronized with the other device the next time they are connected.

✔ **Game Center:** Apple's social networking app for game enthusiasts. Compare achievements, boast of your conquests and high scores, or challenge your friends to battle. (Find out more in Chapter 6.)

✔ **iTunes:** Tap this puppy to purchase music, movies, TV shows, audiobooks, and more, and also download free podcasts and courses from iTunes U. (See Chapter 5 to learn more.)

✔ **App Store:** This icon enables you to connect to and search the iTunes App Store for iPad applications that you can purchase or download for free. (See Chapter 6 to find out more.)

✔ **Newsstand:** Peruse your newspaper and magazine subscriptions, automatically updated of course! Head to Chapter 5 for more details.

✔ **FaceTime:** Tap this icon to start a two-way video chat with a Mac computer, another iPad 2, an iPod touch or an iPhone 4 or 4S. We cover FaceTime like a blanket in Chapter 5.

✔ **Camera:** This icon opens the iPad 2 Camera application, which lets you take still photographs and video clips. Again, Chapter 5 has the inside information on using the Camera app.

✔ **Photo Booth:** Remember those coin-operated photo booth at arcades and carnivals? This application allows you to take photos with all sorts of special effects.

✔ **Settings:** This is where you change settings for your iPad and its apps.

✔ **Safari:** Safari is your Web browser. If you're a Mac user, you know that already. Chapter 4 shows you how to start using Safari on your iPad.

✔ **Mail:** This application lets you send and receive e-mail with most e-mail systems. Chapter 4 helps you start e-mailing from your iPad.

✔ **Photos:** This is the iPad's terrific photo manager. You can view pictures that you've taken on your iPad 2 or transferred from your computer (as well as those transferred from your camera or SD card reader using the optional Camera Connection Kit). iCloud can also deliver new photos from your Mac's iPhoto library using PhotoStream. You can zoom in or out, create slideshows, e-mail photos to friends, and much more.

✔ **Music:** Last but not least, this icon unleashes all the power of an iPod right on your iPad so that you can listen to music or podcasts. Discover how it works in Chapter 5.

Chapter 2

Mastering Multitouch

. . . .

In This Chapter

▶ Mastering multitouch

▶ Cutting, copying, and pasting

▶ Multitasking with your iPad 2

▶ Using folders to get organized

▶ Printing from your iPad 2

▶ Spotlighting search

. . . .

*I*f you already own an iPhone or its close relative, Apple's iPod touch, you have a gigantic start in mastering the iPad multitouch method of navigating the interface with your fingers. If you're a total novice, don't fret. Nothing about multitouch is painful.

Until the original iPad came along, almost every computer known to humankind has had a physical mouse (or trackpad) and a typewriter-style QWERTY keyboard to help you accomplish most of what you do on a computer.

The iPad, like the iPhone, dispenses with a physical mouse and keyboard. Indeed, the iPad (and iPhone) remove the usual physical buttons in favor of a *multitouch display*. And this beautiful and responsive finger-controlled screen is at the heart of the many things you do on the iPad. In the following sections, you discover how to move around the multitouch interface with ease.

Training Your Digits

Rice Krispies has Snap! Crackle! Pop! Apple's response for the iPad is Tap! Flick! Pinch! Oh yeah, and drag.

Fortunately, tapping, flicking, pinching, and dragging are not challenging gestures, so you can master many of these features in no time:

- **Tap:** Tapping serves multiple purposes. Tap an icon to open an application from the Home screen. Tap to start playing a song or choose the photo album you want to look through. Sometimes, you double-tap (tapping twice in rapid succession), which has the effect of zooming in (or out) of Web pages, maps, and e-mails.

- **Flick (sometimes called swipe):** Flicking is just what it sounds like. A flick of the finger on the screen itself lets you quickly scroll through lists of songs, e-mails, and picture thumbnails. Tap on the screen to stop scrolling, or merely wait for the scrolling list to stop.

- **Pinch/spread:** Place two fingers on the edges of a Web page or map or picture, and then spread your fingers apart to enlarge the images. Or, pinch your fingers together to make the map or picture smaller.

- **Drag:** Here's where you slowly press your finger against the touchscreen without lifting it. You might drag to move around a Web page or map that's too large for the iPad's display area.

Navigating beyond Home

The Home screen (refer to Chapter 1) is not the only screen of icons on your tablet. After you start adding apps from the App Store (on your iPad) or the iTunes

App Store (on your computer, which you discover in Chapter 6), you may see two or more tiny dots between the Safari, Mail, Photos, and iPod icons and the row of icons directly above them, plus a tiny Spotlight search magnifying glass to the left of the dots. Those dots denote additional screens, each containing up to 20 additional icons, not counting the four to six separate icons that are docked at the bottom of each of these screens.

To navigate between screens, either flick your finger from right to left or left to right across the middle of the screen, or tap directly on the dots. You can also drag your finger in either horizontal direction to get to a different screen.

 Unlike flicking — you may prefer the term *swiping* — dragging your finger means keeping it pressed against the screen until you get to the page you want.

 You must be very precise, or you'll open one of the application icons instead of switching screens.

The number of dots you see represents the current number of screens on your iPad. The dot that's all white denotes the screen you're currently viewing. Finally, the four icons in the bottom row — Safari, Mail, Photos, and Music — are in a special part of the screen known as the *dock*. When you switch from screen to screen as we described earlier, these icons remain on the screen. In other words, only the first 20 icons on the screen change when you move from one screen to another. You can add one or two more icons to the dock if you so choose. Or move one of the four default icons into the main area of the Home screen to make space available for additional app icons you may use more often.

Press the Home button to jump back to the Home screen.

Here's another multitouch gesture that's new with iOS 5: If you've populated your iPad with several screens of apps, you can also pinch the background to return to the Home screen.

The Incredible Virtual Keyboard

Instead of a physical keyboard, several "soft" or "virtual" English-language keyboard layouts slide up from the bottom of the iPad screen, all variations on these three: the alphabetical keyboard, the numeric and punctuation keyboard, and the more punctuation and symbols keyboard. Figure 2-1 shows the three most common examples of iPad keyboards.

Indeed, the beauty of a software keyboard is that you see only the keys that are pertinent to the task at hand. The layout you see depends on the application. The keyboards in Safari differ from the keyboards in Notes. For example, while having a dedicated *.com* key in the Safari keyboard makes perfect sense, having such a key in the Notes keyboard isn't essential.

Before you consider how to actually *use* the keyboard, we'd like to share a bit of the philosophy behind its so-called *intelligence*. Knowing what makes this keyboard smart can help you make it even smarter when you use it:

- ✔ Includes a built-in English dictionary that even includes words from today's popular culture.

- ✔ Adds your contacts to its dictionary automatically.

- ✔ Uses complex analysis algorithms to predict the word you're trying to type.

- ✔ Suggests corrections as you type. It then offers you the suggested word just below the misspelled word. When you decline a suggestion and the word you typed is *not* in the iPad dictionary, the iPad adds that word to its dictionary and offers it as a suggestion if you mistype a similar word in the future.

Remember to *decline* suggestions (by tapping the characters you typed as opposed to the suggested words that appear beneath what you've typed), because doing so helps your intelligent keyboard become even smarter.

Alphabetical keyboard

Numeric and Punctuation keyboard

More punctuation and symbols keyboard

Figure 2-1: Three faces of the iPad keyboard.

✔ Reduces the number of mistakes you make as you type by intelligently and dynamically resizing the touch zones for certain keys.

Discovering the special-use keys

The iPad keyboard contains several keys that don't actually type a character. Here's the scoop:

 Shift: If you're using the alphabetical keyboard, the Shift key (arrow pointing up) switches between uppercase and lowercase letters. You can tap the key to change the case, or hold down Shift and slide to the letter you want to be capitalized.

 #+= or 123: If you're using keyboards that just show numbers and symbols, the traditional Shift key is replaced by a key labeled #+= or 123 (sometimes shown as .?123). Pressing that key toggles between keyboards that just have symbols and numbers. Press the ABC key to return to the alphabetical keyboard.

 Caps Lock: To turn on Caps Lock and type in all caps, you first need to enable Caps Lock (if not already enabled). You do that by tapping the Settings icon (usually found on the Home screen), then tapping General, and then tapping Keyboard. Tap the Enable Caps Lock item to turn it on. After the Caps Lock setting is enabled, you double-tap the Shift key to turn on Caps Lock. Tap the Shift key again to turn off Caps Lock. To disable Caps Lock completely, just reverse the process by turning off the Enable Caps Lock setting (tap Settings⇨General⇨Keyboard).

 International Keyboard: Only shows up if you've turned on an international keyboard.

Delete: Otherwise known as Backspace, tapping this key erases the character immediately to the left of the cursor.

 Return: Moves the cursor to the beginning of the next line.

 Hide Keyboard: Tap this icon to hide the keyboard. Tap the screen to bring back the keyboard.

Finger-typing on the virtual keyboards

If you're patient and trusting, in a week or so, you'll get the hang of finger-typing. As we've already noted, Apple has built intelligence into its virtual keyboard, so it can correct typing mistakes on the fly and take a stab at predicting what you're about to type next.

As you start typing on the virtual keyboard, we think you'll find the following tips extremely helpful:

- ✓ **See what letter you're typing.** As you press your finger against a letter or number on the screen, the individual key you press darkens until you lift your finger, as shown in Figure 2-2.

- ✓ **Slide to the correct letter if you tap the wrong one.** No need to worry if you touched the wrong key. You can slide your finger to the correct key because the letter isn't recorded until you release your finger.

- ✓ **Tap and hold to access special accent marks (or in Safari, Web address endings).** Sending a message to an overseas pal? Keep your finger pressed against a letter, and a row of keys showing variations on the character for foreign alphabets pops up, as shown in Figure 2-3. This lets you add the appropriate accent mark. Just slide your finger until the key with the relevant accent mark is pressed.

Meanwhile, if you press and hold the .com key in Safari, it offers you the choice of .com, .net, .edu, or .org.

Figure 2-2: The ABCs of virtual typing.

✔ **Tap the Space key to accept a suggested word, or tap the suggested word to decline the suggestion.** Say that you meant to type a sentence in the Notes application that reads, "I am typing an important . . ." Because of the way your

fingers struck the virtual keys, you actually
entered "I am typing an *importsnt . . .*"
Fortunately, Apple knows that the *a* you meant
to press is next to the *s* that showed up on the
keyboard, just as *t* and *y* and *e* and *r* are side by
side. So the software determines that *important*
was indeed the word you had in mind and
places it in red under the suspect word. To
accept the suggested word, merely tap the
Space key. If for some reason you actually did
mean to type *importsnt*, tap that word to decline
the suggested alternative.

If you don't appreciate this feature, you can turn
off Auto-Correction in Settings.

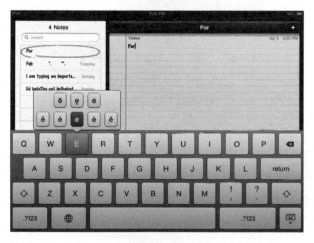

Figure 2-3: Accenting your letters.

Because Apple knows what you're up to, the virtual keyboard is fine-tuned for the task at hand.
This is especially true when you need to enter
numbers, punctuation, or symbols:

✔ **Finding keys for Web addresses:** If you're entering a Web address, the keyboard inside the Safari Web browser (Chapter 4) includes dedicated period, forward slash, and .com keys but no Space key.

If you're using the Notes application, the keyboard does have a Space key.

✔ **Putting the @ in an e-mail address:** If you're composing an e-mail message (Chapter 4), a dedicated @ key pops up on the keyboard.

✔ **Switching from letters to numbers:** To type a number, symbol, or punctuation mark, tap the 123 key to bring up an alternative virtual keyboard. Tap the ABC key to return to the first keyboard.

✔ **Adding apostrophes:** If you press and hold the Exclamation Mark/Comma key on the iPad, it changes to an apostrophe.

Editing mistakes

It's a good idea to type with abandon and not get hung up over mistyped characters. The self-correcting keyboard can fix many errors. That said, plenty of typos are likely to turn up, especially in the beginning, and you have to correct them manually.

A neat trick for doing so is to hold your finger against the screen to bring up the magnifying glass shown in Figure 2-4. Use it to position the pointer to the spot where you need to make the correction. Then use the Backspace key to delete the error, and press whatever keys you need to type the correct text.

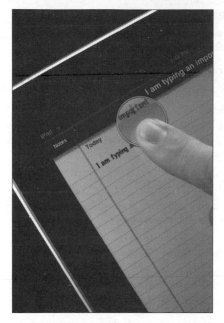

Figure 2-4: Magnifying errors while typing in Notes.

Select, cut, copy, and paste

On the iPad, you can copy, cut, and paste text with pizzazz. You might want to copy text or images from the Web and paste them into an e-mail or a note. Or, you might copy a bunch of pictures or video into an e-mail.

Say you're jotting down ideas in the Notes application that you'll eventually copy into an e-mail. Here's how to exploit the copy-and-paste feature, using this scenario as an example:

1. **Single-tap a word to select it.**

2. **Tap Select to select the adjacent word or tap Select All to grab everything.**

   You can also drag the blue grab points or handles to select a larger block of text or to contract the text you've already selected. This too may take a little practice.

3. **After you've selected the text, tap Copy (see Figure 2-5). If you want to delete the text block, tap Cut instead.**

   You can also select Replace to substitute for the words you've selected.

4. **Now open the Mail program (Chapter 4) and start composing a message.**

5. **When you decide where to insert the text you just copied, tap the cursor.**

   Up pops commands to Select, Select All, and Paste, as shown in Figure 2-6.

6. **Tap Paste to paste the text into the message.**

 Here's the pizzazz part. If you made a mistake when you were cutting, pasting, or typing, shake the iPad. It undoes the last edit.

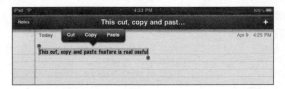

Figure 2-5: Drag the grab points to select text.

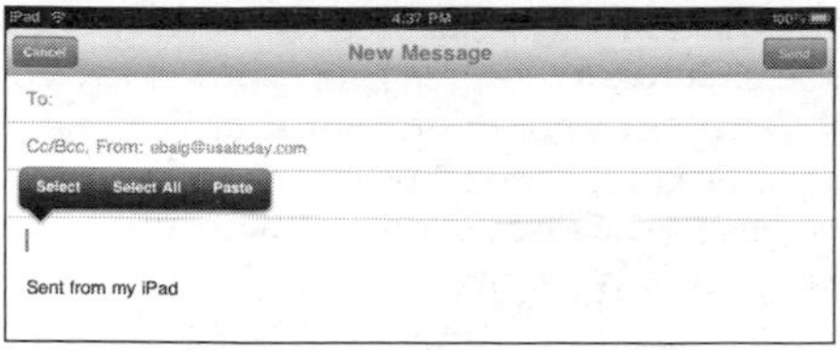

Figure 2-6: Tap Paste to make text appear from nowhere.

Multitasking

iOS 5 software includes multitasking features that make it easy to handle multiple tasks at one time. *Multitasking* simply lets you run numerous apps in the background simultaneously or easily switch from one app to another. For example, a third-party app such as Slacker continues to play music while you surf the Web, peek at pictures, or check e-mail. Without multitasking, Slacker would shut down the moment you opened another app. (Previously, Apple did let you multitask by, for example, playing audio in the background with its own Music app. But multitasking was limited to Apple's own apps, not those produced by outside developers.)

Among other tricks, the multitasking feature lets a navigation app update your position while you're listening, say, to Pandora Internet radio. From time to time, the navigation app will pipe in with turn-by-turn directions, lowering the volume of the music so you can hear the instructions.

And if you're uploading images to a photo Web site and the process is taking longer than you'd like, you can switch to another app, confident that the images will continue to upload behind the scenes. We've also been able to leave voice notes in the Evernote app while checking out a Web page.

Multitasking couldn't be simpler. Double-press the Home button — or use the new gesture, swiping upward with four or five fingers — and a tray appears at the bottom of the screen, as shown in Figure 2-7. The tray holds icons for the most recently used apps. Swipe from right to left on the tray to see more apps. Tap the app you want to switch to; the app remembers where you left off.

Figure 2-7: A tray for recently used apps

Or swipe the tray from left to right for instant access to convenient controls for iPod audio (Volume, Play/Pause, Next/Previous Track), Brightness, and Screen Rotation Lock.

 To remove an app from the tray holding icons of the most recently used apps — and thus remove the app from those in the multitasking rotation — press and hold your finger against any app until they all start to wiggle. Then tap the red circle with the white line that appears inside the app you want to remove. Poof, it's gone.

 Multitasking on the iPad differs from multitasking on a PC or a Mac. You can't display more than one screen at a time. Moreover, there's some philosophical debate whether this feature is multitasking, fast task switching, or a combination. Rather than getting bogged down in the semantics, we're just glad that multitasking, or whatever you want to call it, is here and convenient to use.

Organizing Icons into Folders

Finding the single app you want to use among apps spread out over 11 pages may seem like a daunting task. But Apple felt your pain and includes a handy organizational tool called Folders. The Folders feature lets you create folder icons, each with up to 20 icons for apps.

To create a folder, press your finger against an icon until all the icons on the screen jiggle. Decide which apps you want to move to a folder, and drag the icon for the first app on top of the second app. The two apps now share living quarters inside a newly created folder, as shown in Figure 2-8. Apple names the folder according to the category of apps inside the folder, but you can easily change the folder name by tapping the X in the bar where the folder name appears and substituting a new name.

Figure 2-8: Dragging one app on top of another creates a folder.

To launch an app that's inside a folder, tap that folder's icon and then tap the icon for the app that you want to open. You can drag apps into and out of any folder as long as there's room for them. When you drag all the apps from a folder, the folder disappears automatically.

Printing

Apple didn't include built-in printer functionality when the iPad first came out. With the addition of the AirPrint feature, however, you can print wirelessly from the iPad to an AirPrint-capable printer. The first of these compatible printers emerged on a wide range of HP models, and a number of Canon Wi-Fi printers now offer the feature. The expectation is that other printer manufacturers will unveil AirPrint printers of their own perhaps by the time you read this. AirPrint works (as of this writing) with Mail, Photos, Safari, iBooks (PDFs), and third-party apps that include printing support. You can also print from apps in Apple's optional iWork software suite.

To print, tap the Print command, which appears in different places depending on the app you're using. Then tap Select Printer to select a printer, which the iPad should locate in short order. Depending on the printer, you can specify the number of copies you want to print, the number of double-sided copies, and a range of pages to print.

 Although AirPrint printers don't need any special software, they do have to be connected to the same Wi-Fi network as the iPad.

If you happen to double-click the Home button while a print job is underway, the Print Center app icon appears on the multitasking tray along with all your other recently used apps. A red badge indicates how many documents are in the print queue, along with the currently printing document. Tap the Print Center icon to display additional information about the document that's currently printing, or to cancel the printing of the current document.

Searching for Content

Searching across the iPad is based on the powerful Spotlight feature familiar to Mac owners. Here's how it works:

1. **To access Spotlight, flick to the left of the main Home screen.**

2. **In the bar at the top of the screen that slides into view, enter your search query using the virtual keyboard.**

   The iPad starts spitting out results the moment you type a single character, and the list gets narrowed as you type additional characters.

   The results are pretty darn thorough. Say you entered **Ring** as your search term. Contacts whose last names have *Ring* in them show up, along with friends who might do a trapeze act in the Ringling Bros. circus. All the songs on your iPad by Ringo Starr show up too, as do such song titles as Tony Bennett's "When Do The Bells Ring For Me," if that happens to be in your library. Same goes for apps with the word *Ring*.

3. **Tap any listing to jump to the contact, ditty, or application you're searching for.**

In Settings, you can specify the order of search results so that apps come first, contacts second, songs third, and so on. Within Settings, tap General➪Spotlight Search.

Chapter 3

Getting Stuff to and from Your iPad

● ●

In This Chapter

▶ Starting your first sync

▶ Disconnecting during a sync

▶ Synchronizing contacts, calendars, e-mail accounts, and bookmarks

▶ Synchronizing apps, music, videos, and other media

▶ Configuring and using the Notification Center

● ●

*T*he good news is that you can easily copy any or all of your contacts, calendars, mail settings, bookmarks, books, music, movies, TV shows, podcasts, photos, and applications from your computer to your iPad. The more good news is that all that data is kept up to date automatically in both places whenever you make a change in one place or the other. So when you add or change a calendar, or a contact on your iPad, that information automatically appears on your computer the next time your iPad and computer communicate wirelessly through iCloud.

In the same manner, any apps, music, books, videos or movies you purchase through the iTunes Store can be downloaded to your iPad automatically.

This automatic wireless communication via iCloud between your iPad and computer is called *pushing*, but you can also transfer data the old-fashioned way: by *syncing* (short for synchronizing) using the USB cable that accompanied your iPad. Don't worry: It's easy, and we're going to walk you through the entire process in this chapter.

 The information in this chapter is based on iTunes version 10.5 and iPhone OS version 5.0, which were the latest and greatest when these words were written.

We'll also introduce you to one of the brand-new features within iOS 5: the Notification Center, which gathers all of the notifications from your applications in one convenient, easy-to-use location.

Starting to Sync

Synchronizing your iPad with your computer over a USB cable connection is a lot like syncing an iPod or iPhone with your computer. If you're an iPod or iPhone user, the process will be a familiar piece of cake. But it's not too difficult even for those who've never used an iPod, an iPhone, or iTunes. (Don't forget, many of the steps in the following process only occur the first time you sync your iPad — in fact, you may only need to sync using a cable once!)

First, make sure you've installed iTunes on your Mac or PC (if you need to download it, visit www.apple. com for your own free copy). Once you've installed iTunes, follow these steps:

1. **Connect your iPad to your computer with the USB cable that came with your iPad.**

   When you connect your iPad to your computer, iTunes should start automatically. If iTunes

doesn't start automatically, try running it
manually.

2. Select your iPad in the iTunes sidebar.

You see the Welcome pane, as shown in Figure 3-1.

 If you don't see an iPad in the sidebar (at the left
side of the iTunes window), and you're sure it's
connected to a USB port on your computer (not the
keyboard, monitor, or hub), restart your computer.

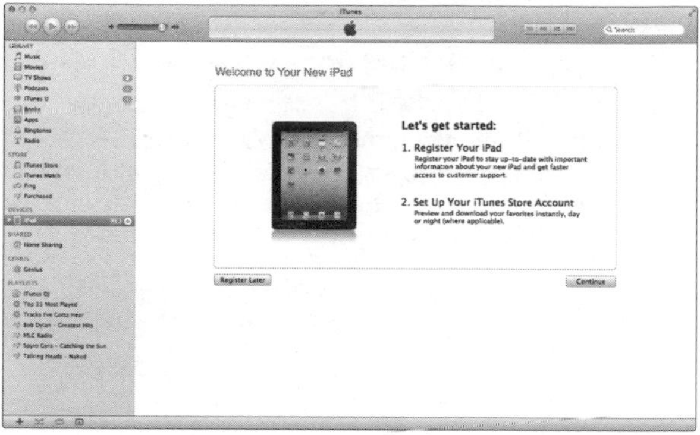

Figure 3-1: This is the first thing you see in iTunes.

3. Click Continue.

iTunes presents the inevitable license agreement.
After you've read the entire tome, click the I Have
Read and Agree check box to select it and click
Continue.

4. Enter (or create) your Apple ID and password.

If you've used the iTunes Store or previously reg-
istered an Apple product, just type your ID and
password — otherwise, follow the directions for
creating an Apple ID. Once you've entered your
ID, click Continue.

5. **Enter your registration information.**

   Once you've entered everything, click Submit to register.

6. **(Optional) Set up Find My iPad.**

   This feature helps you locate your iPad if it's lost or stolen. If you do decide to use this feature, click Set up Find My iPad to display the instructions. To skip this step, click Not Now.

7. **Name your iPad by typing a name in the Name text box.**

8. **After you click the Done button, the Summary pane should appear.**

   If the Summary pane doesn't appear, be sure your iPad is still selected on the left side of the iTunes window. Then click the Summary tab near the top of the window, as shown in Figure 3-2.

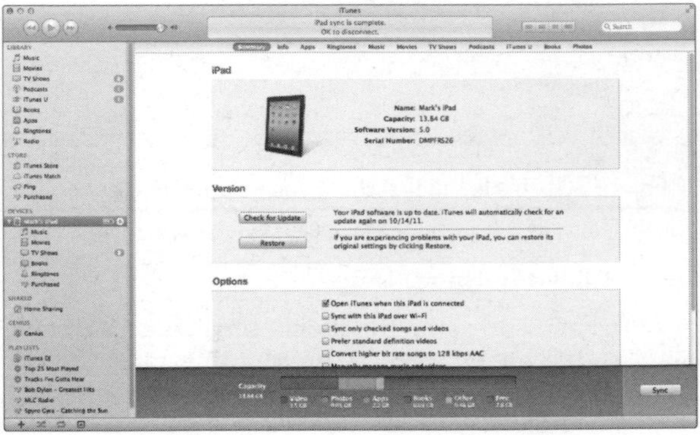

Figure 3-2: The Summary pane is pretty painless.

9. **If you want iTunes to launch automatically whenever you connect your iPad to your computer, click to put a check mark in the Open**

iTunes When This iPad Is Connected check box (in the Options area).

 If you do select the Open iTunes When This iPad Is Connected check box but don't want your iPad 2 to sync automatically every time it's connected, launch iTunes and choose iTunes➪ Preferences (Mac) or Edit➪Preferences (Windows). Click the Devices tab at the top of the window and select the Prevent iPods, iPhones, and iPads from Syncing Automatically check box. If you choose this option, you can sync your iPad by clicking the Sync or Apply button that appears in the lower-right corner of the iTunes window when your iPad is selected in the sidebar (it says Sync in Figure 3-2).

10. **To sync automatically with your computer over a Wi-Fi connection, select the Sync with this iPad over Wi-Fi.**

    Note that enabling this option will still allow your computer to sync with your iPad when connected with the USB cable. Also, your iPad must be connected to a power source and connected to a Wi-Fi network for Wi-Fi syncing to work.

 You can also configure your iPad to allow automatic downloads of music, apps and books that you install on other iOS 5 devices. Tap the Settings icon on the Home screen, then tap Store in the list at the left of the Settings screen. Enable each of the media types that you want to automatically receive on your iPad.

11. **If you want to sync only items that have check marks to the left of their names in your iTunes library, select the Sync Only Checked Songs and Videos check box.**

12. **If you want high-definition videos you import to be automatically converted into smaller standard-definition video files when you transfer**

them to your iPad, select the Prefer Standard Definition Videos check box.

Standard-definition video files are significantly smaller than high-definition video files. You'll hardly notice the difference when you watch the video on your iPad but you'll be able to have more video files on your iPad because they take up less space.

 The conversion from HD to standard definition takes a long time; be prepared for very long sync times when you sync new HD video and have this option enabled.

13. **If you want songs with bit rates higher than 128 kbps converted into smaller 128-kbps AAC files when you transfer them to your iPad, select the Convert Higher Bit Rate Songs to 128 kbps AAC check box.**

A higher bit rate means that the song will have better sound quality but use a lot of storage space. Songs that you buy at the iTunes Store or on Amazon.com, for example, have bit rates of around 256 kbps. So, a 4-minute song with a 256-kbps bit rate is around 8MB; convert it to 128-kbps AAC and it will be roughly half that size (that is, around 4MB), while sounding almost as good.

14. **If you want to turn off automatic syncing in the Music and Video panes, select the Manually Manage Music and Videos check box.**

15. **If you want to password-protect your backups (your iPad creates a backup of its contents automatically every time you sync using the cable), select the Encrypt iPad Backup check box.**

 You can also set your iPad to backup wirelessly using the iCloud Backup feature on your iPad — if you turn iCloud Backup on, iTunes will not back up your iPad data when it's connected by cable. To set things in motion, tap the Settings icon on the Home screen, then tap the iCloud item. Swipe the iCloud Backup switch to turn it on. You can always start an iCloud Backup by tapping the Back Up Now button on this screen. (Remember, however, that your iPad must be plugged in to a power source and must be connected to a Wi-Fi network for an iCloud Backup.)

If you do decide to encrypt your backups, click the Change Password button to enter your own password.

And, of course, if you decide to select the Prevent iPods, iPhones, and iPads from Syncing Automatically check box on iTunes Preferences' Devices tab, you can still synchronize manually by clicking the Sync button in the lower-right corner of the window.

By the way, if you've changed any sync settings since the last time you synchronized, the Sync button instead says Apply.

Disconnecting the iPad

When the iPad is syncing with your computer over a cable connection , its screen says Sync in Progress, and iTunes displays a message that says that it's syncing with your iPad. After the sync is finished, iTunes displays a message that the iPad sync is complete and that it's okay to disconnect your iPad.

If you disconnect your iPad before a sync is completed, all or part of the sync may fail.

To cancel a sync so that you can *safely* disconnect your iPad, drag the slider on the iPad (the one that says *Slide to Cancel*) during the sync.

Synchronizing Your Data

Did you choose to set up data synchronization manually? If you did, your next order of business is to tell iTunes what data you want to synchronize between your iPad and your computer. You do this by selecting your iPad in the sidebar on the left side of the iTunes screen and clicking the Info tab, which is to the right of the Summary tab.

The Info pane has five sections: Contacts, Calendars, Mail Accounts, Other, and Advanced. The following sections look at these sections one by one.

iCloud

iCloud is Apple's new free service for keeping your iPad, iPod touch, iPhone, Macs, and PCs synchronized. It is the latest iteration of what Apple used to call MobileMe. The big allure of iCloud is that it can "push" information, such as e-mail, calendars, contacts, and bookmarks from your computer to and from your iPad and keep those items synchronized on your iPad and computer(s) wirelessly and without human intervention. Plus, iCloud allows you to re-download apps, music, and video that you've bought from the iTunes Store and App Store at any time.

If you're going to use iCloud, you can safely ignore the information in the "Advanced" section, which deals with replacing specified information on your iPad during a single synchronization.

Contacts

The Contacts section of the Info pane determines how iTunes handles synchronization for your contacts. One method is to synchronize all your contacts, as shown in Figure 3-3. Or, you can synchronize any or all groups of contacts you've created in your computer's address book program. Just select the appropriate check boxes in the Selected Groups list, and only those groups will be synchronized.

 Note that the section is named Sync Address Book Contacts because Figure 3-3 was captured in iTunes on a Mac, and Address Book is what it syncs with. If you use a PC, you see a drop-down menu that gives you the choice of Outlook, Google Contacts, Windows Address Book, or Yahoo! Address Book. Don't worry — the process works the same on either platform.

The iPad syncs with the following address book programs:

- ✔ **Mac:** Address Book
- ✔ **PC:** Outlook, Google Contacts, Windows Address Book, or Yahoo! Address Book
- ✔ **Mac and PC:** Yahoo! Address Book and Google Contacts

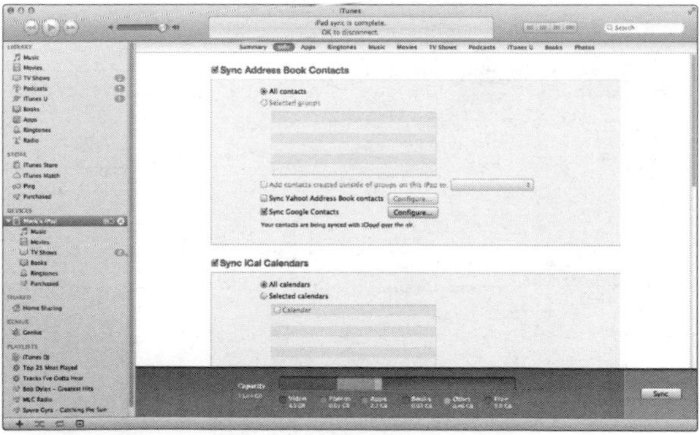

Figure 3-3: This is where you set things up to synchronize your contacts.

If you use Yahoo! Address Book, select the Sync Yahoo! Address Book Contacts check box and then click the Configure button to enter your Yahoo! ID and password. If you use Google Contacts, select the Sync Google Contacts check box and then click the Configure button to enter your Google ID and password.

Calendars

The Calendars section of the Info pane determines how synchronization is handled for your appointments and events. You can synchronize all your calendars, as shown in Figure 3-4. Or, you can synchronize any or all individual calendars you've created in your computer's calendar program. Just select the appropriate check boxes.

 The Calendars section is named Sync iCal Calendars because Figure 3-4 was captured in iTunes for the Mac. If you use a PC, this section will be named Sync Calendars with Outlook. As before, don't worry — regardless of its name, it works the same on either platform.

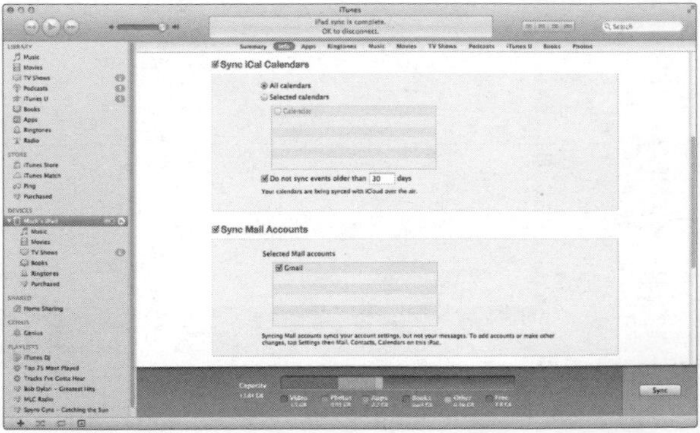

Figure 3-4: Set up sync for your calendar events here.

The iPad syncs with the following calendar programs:

- **Mac:** iCal
- **PC:** Microsoft Outlook 2003 or 2007

Mail accounts

You can sync account settings for your e-mail accounts in the Mail Accounts section of the Info pane. You can synchronize all your e-mail accounts (if you have more than one), or you can synchronize individual accounts, as shown in Figure 3-5. Just select the appropriate check boxes.

The iPad syncs with the following mail programs:

- **Mac:** Mail
- **PC:** Microsoft Outlook 2003 or 2007

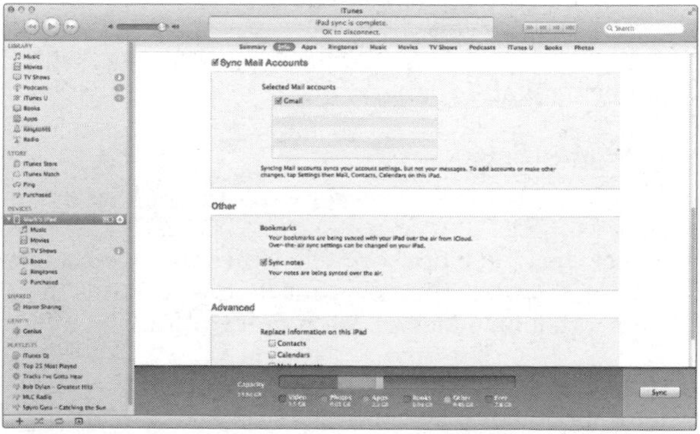

Figure 3-5: Transfer e-mail account settings to your iPad here.

E-mail account settings are synchronized only one way: from your computer to your iPad. If you make changes to any e-mail account settings on your iPad, the changes will *not* be synchronized back to the e-mail account on your computer. Trust us, this is a very good feature and we're glad Apple did it this way.

By the way, the password for your e-mail account may or may not be saved on your computer. If you sync an e-mail account and the iPad asks for a password when you send or receive mail, do this: Tap Settings on the Home screen, tap the Mail, Contacts, Calendars item, tap your e-mail account's name, tap Account, and then type your password in the appropriate field.

Other

The Other section has a mere two items: Sync Safari Bookmarks and Sync Notes.

Select the check box for Sync Safari Bookmarks if you want to sync your Safari bookmarks; don't select it if you don't care about syncing them.

Just so you know, the iPad syncs bookmarks with the following Web browsers:

- **Mac:** Safari
- **PC:** Microsoft Internet Explorer and Safari

Select the check box for Sync Notes to sync notes in the Notes application on your iPad with notes in Apple Mail on a Mac or Microsoft Outlook on a PC.

Note that on a Mac, you must have Mac OS X 10.5.8 or later installed to sync notes.

Synchronizing Your Media

If you chose to let iTunes manage synchronizing your data automatically — either by cable or wire-lessly — welcome. This section looks at how you get your media — your music, podcasts, video, photos and more — from your computer to your iPad.

 Podcasts and video (but not photos) are synced only one way: from your computer to your iPad. Deleting any of these items from your iPad does not delete them from your computer when you sync. The exceptions are songs, podcasts, video, iBooks, and apps that you purchase or download using the iTunes, App Store, or iBooks apps on your iPad, and playlists you create on your iPad. Such items are, as you'd expect, copied back to your computer automatically when you sync. (You can also re-download digital media to your iPad that you've bought through the iTunes Store at any time — iCloud keeps track of everything you've purchased.)

You use the Apps, Ringtones, Music, Podcasts, Movies, TV Shows, Podcasts, iTunes U, Books, and Photos panes to specify the media you want to copy from your computer to your iPad. (Note that some panes won't appear unless you've added that type of media to your library — for example, iTunes U doesn't appear unless you've added something from iTunes U to your iTunes library.) The following sections explain the options you find on each pane.

 To view any of these panes, make sure that your iPad is still selected in the sidebar and then click the appropriate tab near the top of the window.

Apps

If you've downloaded or purchased any iPad apps from the iTunes App Store, set your automatic syncing options as follows:

1. **Click the Apps tab, and then select the Sync Apps check box.**

2. **Choose the individual apps you want to transfer to your iPad by selecting their check boxes.**

   For your convenience, you can sort your applications by name, category, size, kind, or date acquired. Or, you can type a word or phrase into the search field (the oval with the magnifying glass to the right of the words *Sync Apps*) to search for a specific app.

3. **(Optional) Rearrange app icons in iTunes by dragging them where you want them to appear on your iPad, as shown in Figure 3-6.**

4. **Click the Sync or Apply button in the lower-right corner of the window.**

   Your apps are synced and your icons are rearranged on your iPad just the way you arranged them in iTunes.

Screen 1   Screen 2

Icon being dragged to Screen 1

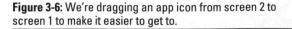

Figure 3-6: We're dragging an app icon from screen 2 to screen 1 to make it easier to get to.

Ringtones

To transfer ringtones to your iPad for use with FaceTime and iMessage, follow these steps:

1. **Click the Ringtones tab and select the Sync Ringtones check box in the Ringtones pane.**

2. **Choose to sync all ringtones or selected ringtones from your iTunes library.**

   Note that the Selected Ringtones option is disabled if you don't have any ringtones in your iTunes library.

3. **If you choose selected ringtones, include them by selecting the appropriate check boxes.**

4. **Click the Sync or Apply button in the lower-right corner of the window.**

   Your ringtones are synced.

Music, music videos, and voice memos

To transfer music to your iPad, follow these steps:

1. **Click the Music tab, and then select the Sync Music check box in the Music pane.**

2. **Select the button for Entire Music Library or Selected Playlists, Artists, Albums, and Genres.**

   If you choose the latter, select the check boxes next to particular playlists, artists, albums, and genres you want to transfer. You can also choose to include music videos or voice memos or both by selecting the appropriate check boxes at the top of the pane (see Figure 3-7).

   If you select the Automatically Fill Free Space with Songs check box, iTunes fills any free space on your iPad with music.

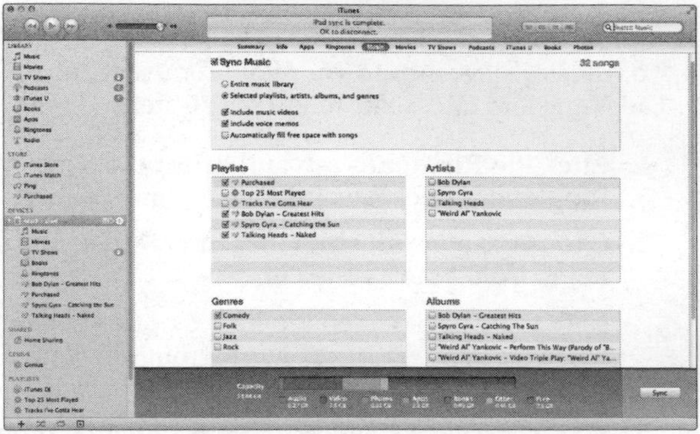

Figure 3-7: Use the Music pane to copy music, music videos, and voice notes from your computer to your iPad.

3. **Click the Sync or Apply button in the lower-right corner of the window.**

   Your music, music videos, and voice memos are synced.

Movies

To transfer movies to your iPad, follow these steps:

1. **Click the Movies tab and select the Sync Movies check box.**

2. **Choose an option for movies that you want to include automatically from the pop-up menu, as shown in Figure 3-8, or select the check box for each movie you want to sync.**

3. **If you also want to include movies within play-lists, select the appropriate check boxes in the Include Movies from Playlists sections of the TV Shows pane.**

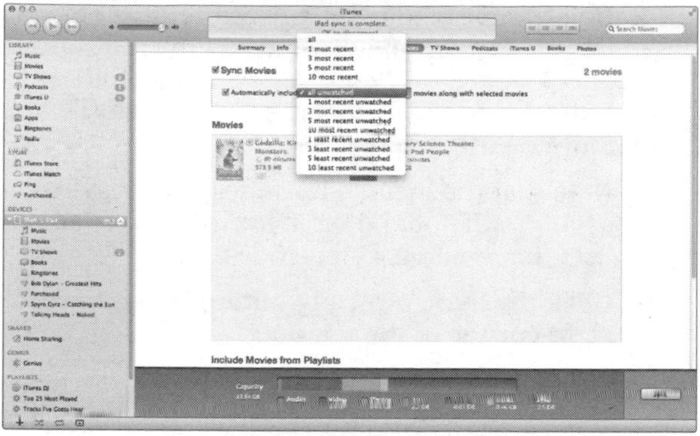

Figure 3-8: Your choices in the Movies pane determine which movies are copied to your iPad.

Note that the Include Movies from Playlists section will not appear if you don't have any playlists that contain TV episodes.

4. **Click the Sync or Apply button in the lower-right corner of the window.**

   Your movies are synced.

TV shows

The procedure for syncing TV shows is slightly different from the procedure for syncing movies. Here's how it works:

1. **Click the TV Shows tab and select the Sync TV Shows check box to enable TV show syncing.**

2. **Choose how many episodes to include from the Automatically Include pop-up menu on the left, as shown in Figure 3-9.**

3. **On the right, choose whether you want all shows or only selected shows.**

4. **If you want to also include individual episodes or episodes on playlists, select the appropriate check boxes in the Episodes and Include Episodes from Playlists sections of the TV Shows pane.**

   Note that the Include Episodes from Playlists section will not appear if you don't have any playlists that contain TV episodes.

5. **Click the Sync or Apply button in the lower-right corner of the window.**

   Your TV shows are synced.

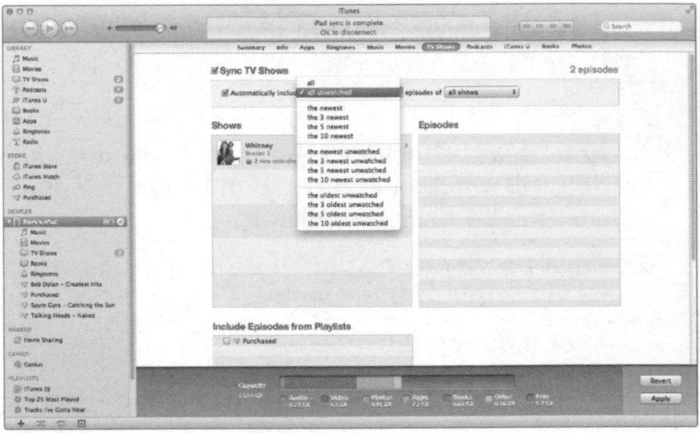

Figure 3-9: These menus determine how TV shows are synced with your iPad.

Podcasts

To transfer podcasts to your iPad, follow these steps:

1. **Click the Podcasts tab and select the Sync Podcasts check box in the Podcasts pane.**

   Two pop-up menus allow you to specify which episodes and which podcasts you want to sync (see Figure 3-10).

2. **Select how many episodes of a podcast you want to sync in the pop-up menu on the left.**

3. **Choose whether to sync all podcasts or just selected podcasts from the pop-up menu in the upper-right corner.**

4. **If you have podcast episodes on playlists, you can include them by selecting the appropriate check box under Include Episodes from Playlists.**

   Note that the Include Episodes from Playlists section will not appear if you don't have any playlists that contain podcast episodes.

5. **Click the Sync or Apply button in the lower-right corner of the window.**

   Your podcasts are synced.

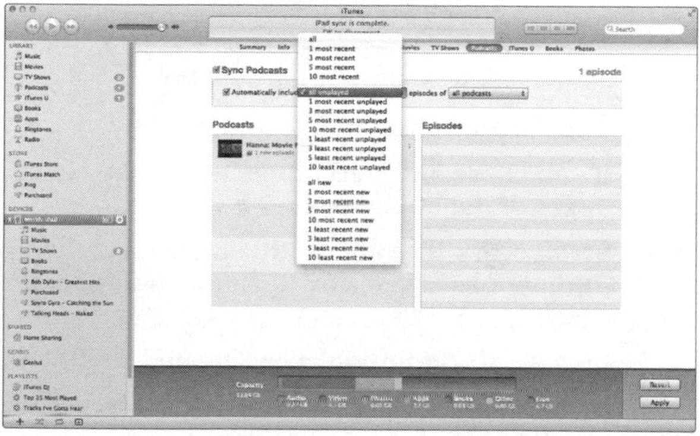

Figure 3-10: These menus determine how podcasts are synced with your iPad.

iTunes U

To sync educational content from iTunes U, follow these steps:

1. Click the iTunes U tab and select the Sync iTunes U check box to enable iTunes U syncing.

2. Choose how many episodes to include.

3. Choose whether you want all collections or only selected collections from the two pop-up menus.

4. If you want to also include individual episodes or episodes on playlists, select the appropriate check boxes in the iTunes U Collections and Items sections of the iTunes U pane.

5. Click the Sync or Apply button in the lower-right corner of the window.

   Your iTunes U episodes are synced.

Books

To sync iBooks and audiobooks, follow these steps:

1. Click the Books tab and select the Sync Books check box to enable book syncing.

2. Choose All Books or Selected Books.

3. If you chose Selected Books, select the check boxes of the books you wish to sync.

4. Scroll down the page a little and select the Sync Audiobooks check box to enable audiobook syncing.

5. Choose All Audiobooks or Selected Audiobooks.

6. If you chose Selected Audiobooks, select the check boxes of the audiobooks you wish to sync.

   If the book is divided into parts, you can select check boxes for the individual parts if you wish.

7. Click the Sync or Apply button in the lower-right corner of the window.

   Your books and audiobooks are synced.

Photos

The iPad syncs photos with the following programs:

- ✔ **Mac:** iPhoto or Aperture
- ✔ **PC:** Adobe Photoshop Album or Adobe Photoshop Elements

You can also sync photos with any folder on your computer that contains images. To sync photos, follow these steps:

1. **Click the Photos tab and select the Sync Photos From check box.**

2. **Choose an application or folder from the pop-up menu (which says iPhoto in Figure 3-11).**

3. **To further refine what photos are synced, you may have any of the following options:**

   - *Select albums, events, and more:* If you choose an application that supports photo albums, events, and/or facial recognition, as we have in Figure 3-11 by choosing iPhoto, you can automatically include events by making a selection from the pop-up menu or select specific albums, events, and/or faces to sync by selecting them in the areas below.

   - *Search for photos to sync:* If you're using iPhoto, you can also type a word or phrase into the search field at the top of the iTunes window (the oval with the magnifying glass) to search for a specific event or events.

   - *Select a folder of images:* If you choose a folder full of images, you can create subfolders inside it that will appear as albums on your iPad.

   But if you choose an application that doesn't support albums or events, or a single folder full of images with no subfolders, you have to transfer all or nothing.

Because we selected iPhoto in the Sync Photos From menu, and iPhoto '11 (the version installed on our Mac) supports events and faces in addition to albums, we also have the option of syncing events, albums, faces, or all three.

4. **Click the Sync or Apply button in the lower-right corner of the window.**

   Your photos are synced.

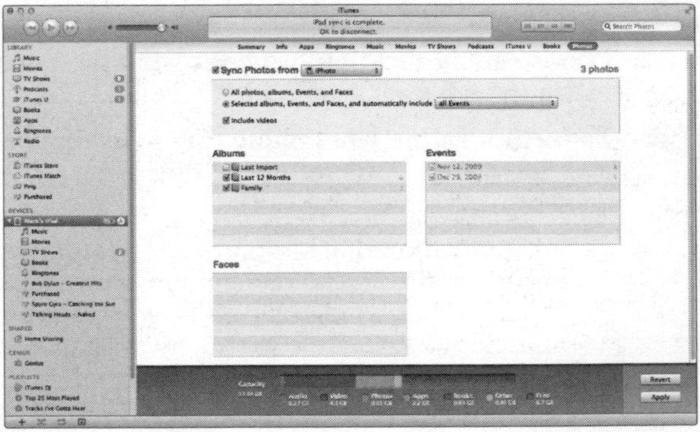

Figure 3-11: The Photos pane determines which photos will be synchronized with your iPad.

Using the Notification Center

With the arrival of iOS 5, Apple debuts a new feature for your iPad: the *Notification Center,* which creates a single spot where you can view all notifications from your iPad apps. Instead of the constant barrage of notification messages displayed by earlier versions of iOS (from games, Mail, Calendar and a host of other apps trying to grab your attention), the Notification Center gathers everything together, and allows you to select which apps can demand your attention.

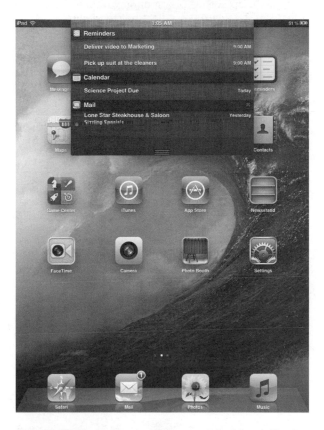

Figure 3-12: The Notification Center puts all of the notification messages from your apps in one list.

To display the Notification Center, swipe downward from the top of any screen. The Center appears in Figure 3-12 — note how multiple notifications are grouped together according to the app that issued them. To open the corresponding item within the app, just tap the desired notification (for example, tapping the notification from the Calendar app opens the corresponding event within Calendar). To close the Notification Center, drag the handle at the bottom (the series of three horizontal lines) up toward the top of the screen.

Naturally, notifications will still appear on your screen as they always have — but with iOS 5, the messages automatically disappear after a short time (and unlike past versions of iOS, the notification text always appears at the top of the screen).

If you still consider notifications as interruptions (and you'd rather do without the distractions), then rejoice: iOS 5 makes it easy to minimize or eliminate them entirely. Tap the Settings icon on the Home screen, then tap the Notifications item in the list at the left side of the screen. Each of the apps that can generate notifications appears in the list on the right — tap the offending app, and you can remove it from the Notification Center entirely. You can also determine the type of alert that app will display (choose the Banners type if you want the message to automatically disappear, or choose None to turn off notifications from that app entirely). To turn off the red badges that appear on the app, disable the Badge App Icon switch. You can also specify whether the app can display messages on your iPad's lock screen.

Chapter 4

Surfing and Sending: Web and Messaging

In This Chapter

▶ Surfing the Net

▶ Opening and displaying Web pages

▶ Using Reminders

▶ Getting e-mail set up

▶ Sending, reading, and managing e-mail

▶ Sending iMessages

*T*he iPad's glorious display, in combination with the powerful new Apple-designed dual-core A5 chip inside the machine, makes browsing on Apple's tablet an absolute delight. In this chapter, you discover the pleasures — and the few roadblocks — in navigating cyberspace on your iPad.

Surfin' Dude

A version of the Apple Safari Web browser is a major reason that the Net on the iPad is very much like the Net you've come to expect on a more traditional computer. Safari for the Mac and for Windows is one of the very best Web browsers in the business.

Exploring the browser

We start your cyberexpedition with a quick tour of the Safari browser. Take a gander at Figure 4-1.

Bookmarks

Previous

Next Page

Go to Add Bookmarks page, Add to Home Screen, Mail Link to this Page or Print

Address field

Search Google or Yahoo!

Reload Web Page

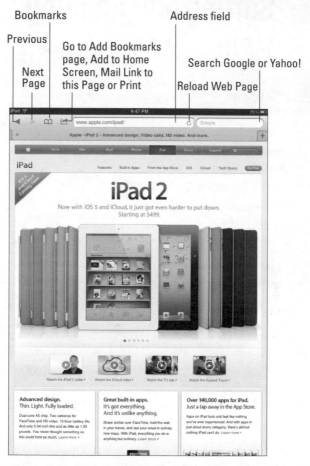

Figure 4-1: The iPad's Safari browser.

Blasting off into cyberspace

Surfing the Web begins with a Web address, of course.
When you tap the address field in iPad's Safari, the
virtual keyboard appears. You may notice one thing
about the keyboard right off the bat. Because so many
Web addresses end with the suffix .com (pronounced
dot com), the virtual keyboard has a dedicated .com
key. For other common Web suffixes — .edu, .net,
and .org — press and hold the .com key and choose
the relevant domain type.

Of equal importance, both the period (.) and the slash
(/) are on the virtual keyboard because you fre-
quently use them when entering Web addresses.

The moment you tap a single letter, you see a list of
Web addresses that match those letters. For example,
if you tap the letter *E* (see Figure 4-2), you see Web
listings for ESPN, eBay, and others.

When you tap a letter, the iPad suggests Web sites
either from the Web sites you already bookmarked
(and synced) from Safari or Internet Explorer on your
computer or from your History list — those cyber-
destinations where you recently hung your hat.

Go ahead and open your first Web page now:

1. **Tap the Safari icon docked at the bottom of the
   Home screen.**
2. **Tap the address field (refer to Figure 4-1).**
3. **Begin typing the Web address on the virtual
   keyboard that slides up from the bottom of the
   screen.**

Figure 4-2: Web pages that match your search letter.

4. **Do one of the following:**

   a. To accept one of the bookmarked (or other) sites that show up on the list, merely tap the name. Safari automatically fills in the address field and takes you where you want to go.

   b. Keep tapping the proper keyboard characters until you enter the complete Web address for the site you have in mind. Next tap the Go key found on the right side of the keyboard.

1 Can See Clearly Now

If you know how to open a Web page (if you don't, read the preceding section in this chapter), we can show you how radically simple it is to zoom in on the pages so that you can read what you want to read and see what you want to see, without enlisting a magnifying glass.

Try these neat tricks:

- ✔ **Double-tap the screen so that portion of the text fills the entire screen.** It takes just a second before the screen comes into focus. By way of example, check out Figure 4-3.

- ✔ **Pinch the page.** Sliding your thumb and index finger together and then spreading them also zooms in and out of a page. Again, wait just a moment for the screen to come into focus.

Figure 4-3: Doing a double-tap dance zooms in and out.

 ✔ **Press down on a page and drag it in all directions, or flick through a page from top to bottom.** You're panning and scrolling, baby.

 ✔ **Rotate the iPad to its side.** Watch what happens to the White House Web site, shown in Figure 4-4. It reorients from portrait to a widescreen landscape view. The keyboard is also wider, making it a little easier to enter a new Web address.

Figure 4-4: Going wide.

Safari on the iPad lets you view multiple web pages simultaneously using tabs — by tapping a tab at the top of the screen, it's easy to switch immediately between pages. After you have one page open, here's how to open additional Web pages in Safari:

1. **Tap the New Tab icon (refer to Figure 4-1) on the right side of the navigation bar at the top of the screen.**

   The New Tab button sports a plus sign. Safari displays a new Untitled tab at the top of the page, as shown in Figure 4-5.

2. **Tap the address field and type a Web address for your new page.**

Figure 4-5: A second tab, all open for business.

To close the tab you're currently viewing, tap the X that appears at the left side of the tab.

Using the Reading List

iOS 5 introduces the Safari Reading List, which allows you to save interesting pages you encounter during a surfing session for later reading. Tap the Action icon at the top of the Safari window — it's the square with the arrow at the left of the address field — and tap Add to Reading List. You can do this as often as you like while surfing.

You'll note that you can also send a Tweet with this page by tapping the Tweet button.

To display the Reading List, tap the Bookmarks icon at the top of the window (it looks like an open book) and choose Reading List. Tap a story to view the page, and the story is automatically removed from the list.

Putting Reminders to Work

It's time to banish that old appointment book (or even worse, that stack of tiny scraps of paper in your wallet or purse). With Reminders, your iPad can hold your to-do list (and keep it updated automatically across all of your iOS devices using iCloud). Reminders works with iCal and Outlook, too, keeping track of events between your computer and your iPad.

To get started, tap the Reminders icon on the Home screen. You'll see the layout shown in Figure 4-6. To add a new reminder for a specific day, tap the day on the calendar to highlight it, then tap the Add icon (which carries a plus sign) at the top right corner of the screen. The virtual keyboard appears, allowing you to type the text of your reminder — when you're finished, tap the Hide Keyboard button at the lower right corner. Now you can tap the item itself, which displays the Details dialog; from here, you can set a reminder and specify whether this is a repeating event.

Once you've taken care of a to-do item, you can tap the check box next to it to indicate that it's been completed. To delete a reminder, display the Details dialog again and tap Delete.

 To search for a specific reminder, tap in the Search Reminders box (next to the magnifying glass) and type the text you want to match.

Figure 4-6: The Reminders screen.

Setting Up Your E-Mail

To use Mail, you need an e-mail address. If you have broadband Internet access (that is, a cable modem, FIOS, or DSL), you probably received one or more e-mail addresses when you signed up. If you're one of the handful of readers who doesn't already have an e-mail account, you can get one for free from Yahoo! (http://mail.yahoo.com), Google (http://mail.google.com), AOL (http://www.aol.com), or numerous other service providers.

Set up your account the easy way

Chapter 3 explains the option of automatically syncing the e-mail accounts on your Windows PC or Mac
with your iPad. If you chose that option, your e-mail
accounts should be configured on your iPad already.
You may proceed directly to the later section
"Darling, You Send Me."

If you haven't yet chosen that option but want to set up
your account now, go to Chapter 3 and read that section, sync your iPad, and then you, too, can proceed
directly to the section "Darling, You Send Me."

Set up your account the less easy way

If you don't want to sync the e-mail accounts on your
computer, you can set up an e-mail account on your
iPad manually. It's not quite as easy as clicking a box
and syncing your iPad, but it's not rocket science either.

If you have no e-mail accounts on your iPad, the first
time you launch Mail you'll be walked through the following procedure. If you have one or more e-mail
accounts on your iPad already and want to add a new
account manually, start by tapping Settings on the
Home screen, and then tap Mail, Contacts, Calendars,
and Add Account.

You should now be staring at the Add Account
screen.

Setting up an e-mail account with Microsoft Exchange, Yahoo! Mail, Google, AOL, or Hotmail

If your account is with Yahoo!, Google (Gmail), AOL,
your company's Microsoft Exchange server, or
Microsoft Hotmail, tap the appropriate button on the
Add Account screen now. If your account is with a

provider other than these five, tap the Other button
and skip ahead to the next section.

Enter your name, e-mail address, and password.
There's a field for a description of this account (such
as work or personal), but it tends to fill in automatically with the same contents in the Address field
unless you tell it differently.

Tap the Next button in the top-right corner of the
screen, and you can specify whether contacts, calendars and reminders from this account should be
included on your iPad. Once you've made your
choices and tapped Save, you're finished. That's all
there is to setting up your account!

Darling, You Send Me

Now that your account or accounts are set up, you
next need to know how to use your iPad to send
e-mail. The following sections examine this process.

Sending an all-text message

To compose a new e-mail message, tap Mail on the
Home screen. What you see next depends on how
you're holding your iPad. In landscape mode (see
Figure 4-7), your e-mail accounts or e-mail folders are
listed in a panel along the left side of screen, with the
actual message filling the larger window on the right.

Compose new message

Reply, forward, or print

Trash message ⌐

Move message ⌐

Tap to see
messages in
accounts

Check for new messages

Figure 4-7: When holding the iPad sideways, Mail looks like this.

When you hold the iPad in portrait mode, the last incoming message fills the entire screen. Figure 4-8 shows this view. You have to tap an Inbox button (in the upper-left corner of the screen) to summon a panel that shows other accounts or message previews. These over lay the message that otherwise fills the screen.

To create a new message, follow these steps:

1. **Tap the Compose New Message button (refer to Figure 4-7).**

Figure 4-8: When holding the iPad in portrait mode, the message fills the screen.

The New Message screen appears, ready for you to start typing the recipient's name.

2. **Type the names or e-mail addresses of the recipients in the To field, or tap the + button to the right of the To field to choose a contact or contacts from your iPad's contacts list.**

3. **Type a subject in the Subject field.**

   The subject is optional, but it's considered poor form to send an e-mail message without one.

4. **Type your message in the message area.**

   The message area is immediately below the Subject field. You have ample space to get your message across.

5. **Tap the Send button in the upper-right corner of the screen.**

Your message wings its way to its recipients almost immediately. If you aren't in range of a Wi-Fi network or the AT&T EDGE or 3G data network when you tap Send, the message is sent the next time you're in range of one of these networks.

Sending a photo with a text message

Sometimes a picture is worth a thousand words. When that's the case, here's how to send an e-mail message with a photo enclosed:

1. **Tap the Photos icon on the Home screen.**

2. **Find the photo you want to send.**

3. **Tap the Action button (which looks like a little rectangle with a curved arrow springing out of it) in the upper-right corner of the screen.**

4. **Tap the Email Photo button.**

   An e-mail message appears on-screen with the photo already attached. In fact, the image appears to be embedded in the body of the message, but the recipient receives it as a regular e-mail attachment.

5. **Address the message and type whatever text you like, as you did for an all-text message in the preceding section, and then tap the Send button.**

Replying to or forwarding an e-mail message

When you receive a message and want to reply to it, open the message and then tap the Reply/Reply All/ Forward button, which looks like a curved arrow at

the upper-right corner of the screen, as shown in
Figure 4-9. Then tap the Reply, Reply All, or Forward
button.

Figure 4-9: Reading and managing an e-mail message.

The Reply button creates a blank e-mail message
addressed to the sender of the original message. The
Reply All button creates a blank e-mail message
addressed to the sender and all other recipients of
the original message, plus CCs. (The Reply All option
only appears if more than one recipient was on the
original e-mail.) In both cases, the subject is retained
with a *Re:* prefix added. So if the original subject was
iPad 2 Tips, the reply's subject is *Re: iPad 2 Tips.*

Tapping the Forward button creates an unaddressed
e-mail message that contains the text of the original
message. Add the e-mail address(es) of the person or
people you want to forward the message to, and then
tap Send. In this case, rather than a *Re:* prefix, the
subject is preceded by *Fwd:.* So this time, the subject
is *Fwd: iPad 2 Tips.*

To send your reply or forwarded message, tap the Send button as usual.

Working with Mail Messages

The first half of the mail equation is sending mail, of course. Now it's time for the second half — receiving and reading the stuff. You can tell when you have *unread* mail by looking at the Mail icon at the bottom of your Home screen. The cumulative number of unread messages appears in a little red circle in the upper-right area of the icon.

 You can also set Mail to display notifications using the new Notification Center. From the Settings screen, tap Notifications, then tap the Mail entry to choose the desired notification type.

Reading messages

To read your mail, tap the Mail icon on the Home screen. Remember that what appears on the screen depends on whether you're holding the iPad in portrait or landscape mode, and what was on the screen the last time you opened the Mail application. Held in landscape mode, you'll see the All Inboxes at the top of the Inboxes section (refer to Figure 4-7), which as its name suggests is a repository for all the messages across all your accounts.

Below the All Inboxes listing are the inboxes for your individual accounts. If you tap the listings here, you'll see any subfolders for each individual account (Drafts, Sent Mail, Trash, and so on). Messages are displayed in threads or conversations making them easy to follow. Follow these steps to read your e-mail:

1. **If the e-mail mailbox you want to see isn't front and center, tap the Accounts button in the upper-left corner of the screen to summon the appropriate one.**

2. **(Optional) Tap the Check for New Messages icon to summon new messages.**

3. **Tap one of the inboxes or accounts to check for any new messages within those mailboxes. To summon the unified inbox, tap All Inboxes instead.**

4. **Tap a message to read it.**

Under a thread, only the first message of the conversation displays in the inbox. Tap that message to reveal the entire back and forth. You can turn message threading off by choosing Settings⇨Mail, Contacts, Calendars⇨Organize By Thread.

Managing messages

Managing messages typically involves either moving the messages to a folder or deleting them. To herd your messages into folders, you have the following options:

✔ **To flag a message or mark it as unread,** tap Edit. In both portrait and landscape, Edit appears at the top of your inbox or another mailbox when those mail folders are selected. After tapping Edit, tap the message you want to mark and tap Mark, then choose whether you want to flag it in the message list (Mail adds a tiny red flag icon) or mark it as unread.

✔ **To file a message in another folder,** tap the File Message icon. When the list of folders appears, tap the folder where you want to file the message.

✔ **To move messages to another folder in bulk,** tap Edit. After tapping Edit, it becomes a Cancel

button and buttons labeled Delete (in red) and
Move (in blue) appear at the bottom of the
screen. Tap the circle to the left of each message you want to move so that a check mark
appears. Tap Move, and then tap the new folder
in which you want those messages to hang out.

✔ **To read a message that you've filed away,** tap
the folder where the message resides, and tap
the header or preview for the message.

✔ **To print a message,** tap the Reply, Forward,
Print button (refer to Figure 4-9) and tap Print.

Delete a message by tapping the Delete Message icon.
You have a chance to cancel in case you tap the
Delete Message icon by mistake. You can delete
e-mail messages without opening them in two ways:

✔ Swipe left or right across the message in its preview pane, and then tap the red Delete button
that appears to the right of the message.

✔ Tap the Edit button, and tap the little circle to
the left of each message you want to remove.
Tapping that circle puts a check mark in it and
brightens the red Delete button at the bottom of
the screen. Tap that Delete button to erase all
messages you checked off. Deleted messages
are moved to the Trash folder.

Doing the iMessage Thing

What if we told you that you can send unlimited text
messages to anyone with an iPad, iPhone or iPod
touch that's running iOS 5? Yes, it's indeed cool, but
wait — what if I also told you it was *free?* (Oh, and
you can also send those old-fashioned SMS text messages too, but we all know how much that costs.)

Welcome to *iMessage,* which is built-in to your iPad's Messages app. With iMessage, you can send text, photos, video, contacts and even your current location to another person, using either a Wi-Fi or 3G cellular connection.

The first time you run Messages, you'll enter the email address that the app will use to send and receive messages. (Note that this email account need not be the same account you use for your Apple ID.) Once Messages has verified the address, you'll see the app's main screen.

To send a message, tap the New Message icon (the square with the pencil) at the top of the screen. You can either type the recipient's email address (using the virtual keyboard shown in Figure 4-10), or tap the round icon with the plus sign to select a contact from your Contacts list. (Note that if your recipient is using an iPhone, you'll be using that person's telephone number within Messages.)

 You can add multiple recipients, just as you can within Mail.

Once you've added all your recipients, tap within the text box (right above the virtual keyboard) and begin typing. You can tap the camera icon next to the text box at any time to add either a photo or video from your existing library on your iPad, or you can shoot a video clip or take a photo immediately.

When you're ready to send the message, tap the Send button. You'll see your conversation take place at the right side of the window. Your message bubbles appear on the right, and your recipient's messages appear on the left (this is very familiar to any Mac owner who's used iChat in the past).

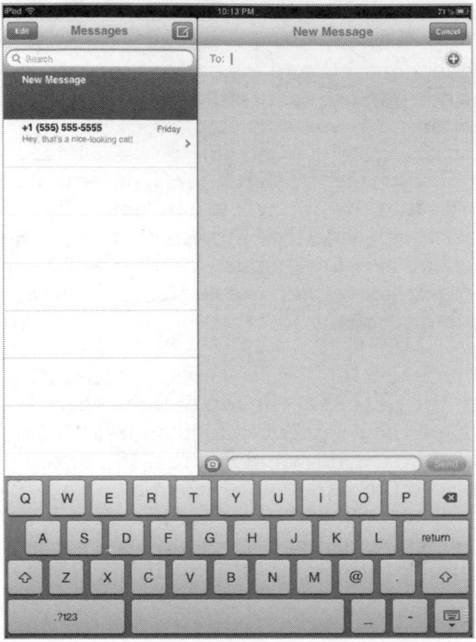

Figure 4-10: Preparing to send an iMessage.

Messages keeps track of your conversations in the list on the left, and you can return to any conversation by tapping it. To delete a conversation, tap the Edit button and tap the red circle icon to the left of the offending conversation, then tap Delete.

Chapter 5

Music, Movies, and Books

In This Chapter

▶ Getting familiar with the iPod inside your iPad

▶ Taking control of your tunes

▶ Finding movies to watch

▶ Chatting with FaceTime

▶ Using the Camera and Photo Booth apps

▶ Shopping the iBookstore

▶ Reading books and periodicals on your iPad

*W*e assume that you have already synced your iPad with your computer and your iPad contains audio content — songs, podcasts, or audiobooks. If you don't have any media on your iPad yet, now is a good time to get some (flip to Chapter 3 and follow the instructions). In this chapter, we show you how to use your iPad 2 to play music and movies, take photos, video chat with friends and family, and read books, newspapers, and magazines.

Introducing the iPod inside Your iPad

To use your iPad as an iPod, just tap the iPod icon on the right side of the dock at the bottom of the screen (unless you've moved it elsewhere).

Here's a quick overview of what you see when the iPod app starts up:

- ✔ **Content window:** Across the majority of the screen, you'll see thumbnails representing your iPad audio library, which contains all the music, podcasts, audiobooks, and playlists you've synced with or purchased on your iPad. You can tap on any of these items.

- ✔ **Player controls:** At the top left corner of the screen, from left to right, you can see the the Rewind/Previous Track button, the Play/Pause button, the Fast Forward/Next Track button, the scrubber bar (for quickly moving through a track) and the volume control.

- ✔ **Playlist and tab navigation:** When you're viewing your library in playlist mode, you can tap the New button (underneath the volume control) to create a new playlist. At the bottom of the screen, from left to right, you can see a button for the iTunes Store, as well as 6 tabs: Playlists, Songs, Artists, Albums and More. (Tap the More button to view Podcasts, Audiobooks, Genres, and Composers).

We will take a closer look at all these features, but for now, Figure 5-1 shows them all.

Playlist thumbnail
Play/Pause   Scrubber/Playhead
Fast Forward   New playlist
Rewind   Repeat   Genius
                              Shuffle   Volume control

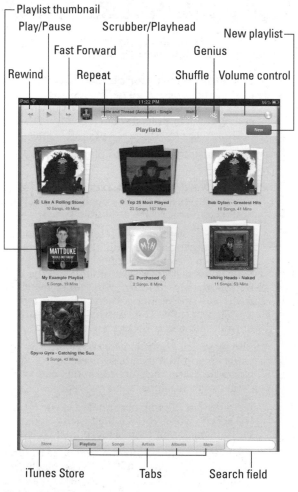

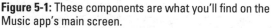

iTunes Store   Tabs   Search field

Figure 5-1: These components are what you'll find on the Music app's main screen.

Playing with the Audio Controls

Take a peek at Figure 5-1 and you can see exactly where all these controls are located on the screen:

- **Rewind/Previous Track button:** When a track is playing, tap once to go to the beginning of the track or tap twice to go to the start of the preceding track in the list. Touch and hold this button to rewind the track at double speed.

- **Play/Pause button:** Tap to play or pause the track.

- **Fast Forward/Next Track button:** Tap to skip to the next track in the list. Touch and hold this button to fast-forward at double speed.

  You can display playback controls anytime a track is playing. Better still, this trick works even when you're using another application or your home screen(s): Just double tap the Home button or swipe upward with four or five fingers to display the Icon tray, then swipe the tray from left to right. The controls appear at the bottom of the screen, as shown in Figure 5-2.

  The playback controls *won't* appear if you're using an app that has its own audio, like many games, any app that records audio, and VoIP (Voice over IP) apps, such as Skype.

  A similar set of controls appears at the *top* of the screen when you double tap the Home button while your iPad is locked.

- **Repeat:** Tap the dual-arrow icon once to repeat all songs in the current list (that is, playlist, album, artist, composer, or genre) and play them all over and over. Tap again to repeat the current song again and again. Tap again to turn off repeat.

Figure 5-2: These controls appear — even if you're using another app — when you double-click the Home button and swipe the tray while a track is playing.

The button appears in black after one tap, in black with a little 1 inside after two taps, and in black and white when repeat is turned off.

✓ **Scrubber bar and playhead:** Drag the little red line (the playhead) along the Scrubber bar to skip to any point within the track.

✓ **Shuffle:** Tap this button (which bears two arrows crossing each other) to play songs at random; tap again to play songs in the order they appear on the screen.

✔ **Volume control:** Drag the dot left or right to
reduce or increase the volume level.

But wait, there's more. You can view the album art
for the current track in a full-screen display — just
tap the album art thumbnail in the Now Playing area
at the top center of the screen. Now, tap anywhere on
the artwork that fills the screen and the familiar controls appear again on the black Now Playing screen,
as shown in Figure 5-3.

Back   Track List

Figure 5-3: You see these additional controls
on the Now Playing area.

The new controls you see are as follows:

> ✔ **Track List:** Tap this button at the lower right of
> the Now Playing screen to see all the tracks on
> the album that contains the song currently play-
> ing, as shown in Figure 5-4.
>
> Tap any song on this list to play it. Or, swipe your
> finger across the dots just beneath the Scrubber
> bar to rate the song from one to five stars. In
> Figure 5-4, we've rated the song four stars.

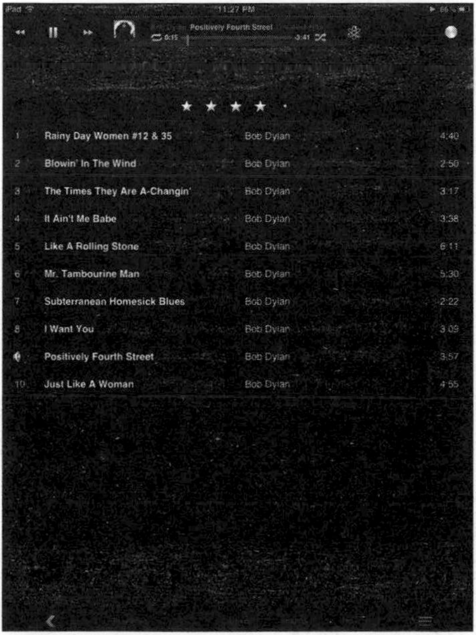

1	Rainy Day Women #12 & 35	Bob Dylan	4:40
2	Blowin' In The Wind	Bob Dylan	2:50
3	The Times They Are A-Changin'	Bob Dylan	3:17
4	It Ain't Me Babe	Bob Dylan	3:38
5	Like A Rolling Stone	Bob Dylan	6:11
6	Mr. Tambourine Man	Bob Dylan	5:30
7	Subterranean Homesick Blues	Bob Dylan	2:22
8	I Want You	Bob Dylan	3:09
9	Positively Fourth Street	Bob Dylan	3:57
10	Just Like A Woman	Bob Dylan	4:55

Figure 5-4: We've given this tune a four-star rating.

Why assign star ratings to songs? One reason is that you can use star ratings to filter songs in iTunes on your Mac or PC. Another is that you can use them when you create Smart Playlists in iTunes. And last but not least, they look cool.

✔ **Back:** Tap this button at the lower-left corner of the Now Playing screen to return to the previous screen.

Using the Genius feature

Genius selects songs from your music library that go great together. To use it, tap the Genius button, and your iPad generates a Genius playlist of songs that it picked because it thinks they go well with the song that's playing.

 To use the Genius feature on your iPad, you need to turn on Genius in iTunes on your computer and then sync your iPad at least one time.

If you tap the Genius button on the main screen (see Figure 5-1) and no song is currently playing, a new Genius playlist thumbnail appears. Tap the Genius playlist thumbnail and you see the songs that Genius selected. Two new buttons appear in the upper-right corner of the list:

✔ **Refresh:** See a list of different songs that "go great with" the song you're listening to (or song you selected).

✔ **Save:** Save this Genius playlist so that you can listen to it whenever you like.

When you save a Genius playlist, it inherits the name of the song it's based upon and appears in your library with a Genius icon that looks like the Genius button. And the next time you sync your iPad 2, the Genius playlist magically appears in iTunes.

Creating playlists

Playlists let you organize songs around a particular theme or mood: operatic arias, romantic ballads, British invasion — whatever. Younger folks sometimes call them *mixes.*

When you click the Playlists button at the bottom of the Music screen, your playlists appear in alphabetical order as thumbnails. And don't worry if you don't have any playlists. Just know that if you had some, you'd see them here.

Although it may be easier to create playlists in iTunes on your computer, your iPad makes it relatively easy to create (and listen to) playlists:

✔ **To create a playlist on your iPad,** click the New button at the upper right (refer to Figure 5-1 for its location). Name your playlist and then tap Save. After you do this, you see a list of the songs on your iPad in alphabetical order. Tap the ones you want to have in this playlist and they turn gray. To add all songs on your iPad, click the Add All Songs button. When you've tapped every song you want in the list, tap the Done button just below the volume control.

✔ **To listen to a playlist,** tap the Playlist button at the bottom of the screen (if necessary) and then tap the desired playlist thumbnail — you see a list of the songs it contains. If the list is longer than one screen, flick upward to scroll down. Tap a song in the list and the song will play. When that song is over or you tap the Next Song button, the next song in the playlist will play. This will continue until the last song in the playlist has played, at which point your iPad will shut up.

Finding Stuff to Watch

You can find and watch videos on your iPad in a couple of different ways. You can fetch all sorts of fare from the iTunes Store, whose virtual doors you can open directly from the iPad. You can download purchases you've made on the iTunes Store using iCloud. Or, you can sync content that already resides on your PC or Mac. (If you haven't done so yet, now is as good a time as any to read Chapter 3 for all the details.)

The videos you can watch on the iPad generally fall into one of the following categories:

- ✔ **Movies, TV shows, and music videos that you purchase or fetch free in the iTunes Store:** You can watch these by tapping the Videos icon on the Home screen.

   The iTunes Store features dedicated sections for purchasing or renting episodes of TV shows (from *Glee* to *Modern Family*), as shown in Figure 5-5, and for buying or renting movies.

   As shown in Figure 5-6, by tapping a movie listing in iTunes, you can generally watch a trailer before buying (or renting) and check out additional tidbits.

- ✔ **The boatload of video podcasts, just about all of them free, featured in the iTunes Store:** Podcasts started out as another form of Internet radio, although instead of listening to live streams, you download files onto your computer or iPod to take in at your leisure. You can still find lots of audio podcasts, but the focus here is on video. You can watch free episodes that cover Sesame Street videos, sports programming, investing strategies, political shows (across the ideological spectrum), and so much more.

Figure 5-5: Buying and watching TV on the iPad is quite modern.

✔ **Videos that play via entertainment apps:** For example, Netflix offers an app that enables you to use your Netflix subscription, if you have one, to stream video on your iPad. Similarly, both ABC and NBC television networks offers appealing apps so that you can catch up on their shows on your iPad.

✔ **Seminars at Harvard, Stanford, or numerous other prestigious institutions:** iTunes University boasts more than 250,000 free lectures from around the world, many of them videos. Better yet, you get no grades, and you don't have to apply for admission, write an essay, or do homework.

Bridesmaids (Unrated) UNRATED HD   Tell a Friend ›

Universal Pictures
Genre: Comedy
Released: 2011
In English
★★★★☆ 865 Ratings

PREVIEW

BUY $19.99   RENT $4.50   HD   SD

Learn About Rentals ›

Plot Summary

"Gut-bustingly funny, Bridesmaids gets an A!!!" (Owen Gleiberman, Entertainment Weekly) From the producer of Superbad, Knocked Up and The 40-Year-Old Virgin comes the breakout comedy critics are calling "brazenly hysterical!" (Alynda Wheat, People) Thirty-something Annie (... **More ▼**

Credits

Actors	Director	Screenwriters	Producers
Kristen Wiig ›	Paul Feig ›	Annie Mumolo ›	Judd Apatow ›
Maya Rudolph ›		Kristen Wiig ›	Clayton Townsend ›
Rose Byrne ›			Barry Mendel ›
Chris O'Dowd ›			
Ellie Kemper ›			
Wendi McLendo...			

Figure 5-6: Bone up on a movie before buying or renting it.

✔ **Homegrown videos from the popular YouTube Internet site:** Apple obviously thinks highly of YouTube because it devoted a dedicated Home screen icon to the site.

✔ **The movies you've created in iMovie software or other software on the Mac or, for that matter, other programs on the PC:** Plus all the other videos you may have downloaded from the Internet.

 You may have to prepare these videos so that they'll play on your iPad. To do so, highlight the video in question after it resides in your iTunes library. Go to the Advanced menu in iTunes, and click Create iPad or Apple TV Version. Alas, this doesn't work for all the video content you download off the Internet, including video files in the AVI, DivX, MKV, and Xvid formats. You need help transferring them to iTunes and converting

them to iPad-friendly formats from other software programs added to your PC or Mac.

Playing Video

Now that you know what you want to watch, here's
how to watch it:

1. **On the Home screen, tap the Videos icon.**

   Videos stored on your iPad are segregated by
   category — Movies, Rented Movies, TV Shows,
   Podcasts, Music Videos, and iTunes U. For each
   category, you see the program's poster art, as
   shown in Figure 5-7. Categories such as Rented
   Movies, Podcasts, and iTunes U only appear if
   you have that type of content loaded on the
   machine.

Movies

TV Shows

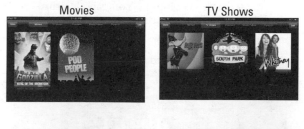

Lectures

Music Videos

Figure 5-7: Choosing the movie, TV show, lecture, or music
video to watch.

2. **At the top of the screen, select the tab that corresponds to the type of video you want to watch.**

3. **Tap the poster that represents the movie, TV show, or other video you want to watch.**

   You see a full description of the movie you want to watch, along with a listing of cast and filmmakers, as shown in Figure 5-8. Tap the Chapters tab to browse the chapters. You see thumbnail images and the length of the chapter. Tap the Info tab to return to a description.

4. **To start playing a movie (or resume playing from where you left off), tap the Play arrow; alternatively, from the Chapters view (see Figure 5-8), tap any chapter to start playing from that point.**

   If you go to Settings from the Home screen and tap Video, you can change the default setting to start playing from where you left off to start playing from the beginning. You can also turn on Closed Captioning for those media types that support it.

Figure 5-8: Start playing from any chapter.

5. **(Optional) Rotate your iPad to landscape mode to maximize a movie's display.**

   For movies, this is a great thing. You can watch flicks as the filmmaker intended, in a cinematic *aspect ratio*.

 By using an Apple Digital AV Adapter and an HDMI cable (or by using AirPlay with an AppleTV unit), your iPad 2 can display the same video on both the built-in screen and a TV with an HDMI port. Tap the Settings icon on the Home screen, and then tap Video to configure your iPad for widescreen display on your TV.

Chatting with a View: FaceTime

One of the great new iPad 2 features is the addition of a front camera and FaceTime, the app that allows you to video chat with other FaceTime users over a Wi-Fi link.

 You need a Wi-Fi connection to use FaceTime — a 3G cellular connection will not work — and the other person must have a Mac computer, an iPad 2, an iPod touch, or an iPhone 4 with FaceTime installed.

The first time you use FaceTime, you must enter your Apple ID and your e-mail address. The folks you chat with on the other end will use your e-mail address to call you via FaceTime.

After you sign in, follow these steps to make a call:

1. **Tap a contact from the list.**

   FaceTime displays your Contacts list by default, but there are other methods of selecting some- one to call. To display a list of recent calls, tap the Recent icon. You can also display a list of your favorite FaceTime callers by tapping the

Favorites icon. To add someone as a favorite, tap the Add button (which carries a plus sign) at the top of the list.

2. **When the call is accepted, you can see video from the caller's location.**

   Speak normally, and your caller should have no problem hearing you.

3. **(Optional) During the call, switch between front and back cameras by tapping the Camera Switch icon.**

   You can use either camera with FaceTime — send video of yourself with the front camera, or share your surroundings while you talk using the back camera.

4. **(Optional) To turn off audio from your side of the call, tap the Mute icon.**

   You can still hear audio from the caller's side of the conversation. Tap the Mute icon again to turn your microphone back on.

 Press the Home button during a call, and you can run another app! You won't see the video, of course, but you can continue talking. Once you're done with the other application, tap the green bar at the top of the window to return to FaceTime.

5. **To hang up and end the call, tap the End icon.**

If someone calls you with FaceTime, your iPad 2 notifies you with a message. You can then choose to accept or dismiss the call.

Shooting Photos and Video

You can use the Camera app to take still photos and video using either of the cameras on the iPad 2. Tap the Camera icon, and you see a real-time display. To switch cameras between front and back, tap the Switch icon in the upper-right corner of the screen. (Remember, you can also change the camera's orientation by simply rotating your iPad 2.) To switch between still photos and video, tap the Photo/Video icon in the lower-right corner of the screen.

When you're ready to shoot, tap the Camera button at the bottom center of the screen. If you're shooting video, tap the Camera button again to stop recording. To review your photos and video clips, tap the Review thumbnail at the bottom left of the screen — you can print and e-mail your handiwork, as well as use photos as wallpaper.

 While reviewing your photos, tap the Slideshow button at the top of the screen for an instant professional-looking slideshow. *Way to go, Apple!*

To add a little spice and special effects to your still photos, tap the Photo Booth icon on the Home screen. You can choose from eight different effects for your images. And again, you can switch between the front and back cameras. Tap the Camera button to shoot some out-of-this-world photos.

Shopping for E-Books

To start reading electronic books on your iPad, you have to fetch the iBooks app from the App Store. As you might imagine, the app is free, and it comes with access to Apple's *iBookstore*. With the iBookstore, Apple makes it a cinch to search for books you want to read, and it even lets you peruse a sample prior to parting with your hard-earned dollars. To enter the store, tap the iBooks icon and then tap the Store button in the upper-left corner of your virtual bookshelf or your library List view.

Browsing the iBookstore

You have several ways to browse for books in the iBookstore. The top half of the screen shows ever-changing ads for books that fit a chosen category. But you can also browse Recent Releases in the particular category you have in mind. The left- and right-pointing arrows (see Figure 5-9) indicate more recent releases to peek at. Or tap See All for many more selections.

Figure 5-9: The featured page for the Humor category.

To choose another category of books, tap the Categories button to summon the list. You have to scroll to see the bottom of the list.

Now look at the bottom of the screen. You see the following icons:

✔ **Featured:** This is where we've been hanging out so far. Featured works are the books being promoted in the store. These may include popular titles from Oprah's Book Club or an author spotlight from the likes of *Twilight* writer Stephenie Meyer.

✔ **NYTimes:** Short for *The New York Times,* of course. These books make the newspaper's famous bestsellers lists, which are divided into fiction and nonfiction works. The top ten books in each list are initially shown. To see more titles, tap Show More at the bottom of the screen. You have to scroll down to see it.

✔ **Top Charts:** Here Apple is showing you the most popular books in the iBookstore. You find a list for Top Paid Books and Top Free Books. Once more, you can see more than the top ten shown in each category by tapping Show More.

✔ **Browse:** Tap this icon to look through the store in a convenient list form (by authors or categories).

✔ **Purchased:** Tapping here shows you the books you've already bought. In this area, you can also check out your iTunes account information, tap a button that transports you to iTunes customer service, and redeem any iTunes gift cards or gift certificates. To re-download a book through iCloud, tap the iCloud icon next to the desired title — you can toggle between a display of all the books you've purchased or a display of only the books that haven't been downloaded on your iPad yet.

Searching the iBookstore

In the upper-right corner of the iBookstore is a search field, similar to the Search field you see in iTunes. Using the virtual keyboard, type in an author name or title to find the book you're looking for.

If you like freebies, search for the word *free* in the iBookstore. You'll find dozens of (mostly classic) books that cost nothing, and you won't even have to import them. See the section "Finding free books outside the iBookstore," later in this chapter, for more places to find free books.

Buying a book from the iBookstore

Assuming that the book exceeds your lofty standards and you are ready to purchase it, here's how to do so:

1. **Tap the price shown in the gray button on the book's information page.**

   Upon doing so, the dollar amount disappears and the button becomes green and carries a Buy Book label. If you tap a free book instead, the button is labeled Get Book.

2. **Tap the Buy Book/Get Book button.**

3. **Enter your iTunes password to proceed with the transaction.**

   The book appears on your bookshelf in an instant, ready for you to tap it and start reading.

Buying books beyond Apple

The business world is full of examples where one company competes with another on some level only to work with it as a partner on another. When the iPad first burst onto the scene in early April 2010, pundits immediately compared it to Amazon's Kindle, the market-leading electronic reader. Sure the iPad had the larger screen and color, but Kindle had a few bragging points too, including longer battery life (up to about two weeks versus about 10 hours for the iPad), a lighter weight, and a larger selection of books in its online bookstore.

But Amazon has long said it wants Kindle books to be available for all sorts of electronic platforms, and the iPad, like the iPhone and iPod touch before it, is no exception. So we recommend taking a look at the free Kindle app for the iPad, especially if you've already purchased a number of books in Amazon's Kindle Store and want access to that wider selection of titles.

Meanwhile, we haven't tried them all, and we know it's hard enough competing against Apple (or Amazon). But we'd be selling our readers short if we didn't at least mention that you can find several other e-book-type apps for the iPad in the App Store. As this book goes to press, you can have a look at the following apps, just to name a few:

- ✔ Cloud Readers from Satoshi Nakajima (free)
- ✔ eBooks by Kobo HD from Indigo Books and Music (free)
- ✔ Read Demon PDF Reader from DeadNick ($4.99)
- ✔ Stanza from Lexcycle (free)

Finding free books outside the iBookstore

Apple supports a technical standard called *ePub,* the underlying technology behind thousands of free public-domain books. You can import these to the iPad without shopping in the iBookstore. Such titles must be *DRM*-free, which means they are free of digital rights restrictions.

To import ePub titles, you have to download them to your PC or Mac (assuming that they're not already there) and then sync them to the iPad through iTunes.

You can find ePub titles at numerous cyberspace destinations, among them

- Feedbooks (www.feedbooks.com)
- Google Books (http://books.google.com/ebooks) (Google has a downloadable app).
- Project Gutenberg (www.gutenberg.us)
- Smashwords (www.smashwords.com)

Reading a Book

Once you've found and downloaded a book, you can start reading by tapping it on the bookshelf in your iPad library. The book leaps off the shelf, and at the same time, it opens to either the beginning of the book or the place where you left off last time. Figure 5-10 shows a title page.

While lounging around reading, and especially if you're lying down, we recommend that you use the screen rotation lock (shown back in Chapter 1) to stop the iPad from inadvertently rotating the display.

You can also take advantage of the iPad's VoiceOver feature to have the iPad read to you out loud. It may not be quite like having Mom or Dad read you to sleep, but it can be a potential godsend to those with impaired vision.

Turn pages

To turn to the *next* page of a book, do any of the following:

- **Tap or flick your finger near the right margin of the page.** If you tap or flick, the page turns in a blink.

- **Drag your finger near the margin,** and the page folds down as it turns, as if you were turning pages in a real book.

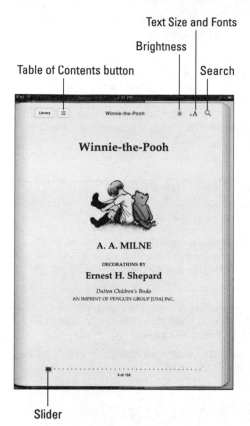

Table of Contents button   Brightness   Search

Text Size and Fonts

Slider

Figure 5-10: Books on the iPad offer handy reading and navigation tools.

> ✔ **Drag down from the upper-right corner of the book,** and the page curls from that spot.
>
> ✔ **Drag up from the lower-right corner,** and it drags up from that spot.
>
> ✔ **Drag from the middle-right margin,** and the entire page curls.

To turn to the *previous* page in a book, tap, flick, or drag your finger in a similar fashion, except now do so closer to the left margin.

 The iPad is smart, remembering where you left off. So if you close a book by tapping the Library button in the upper-left corner or by pressing the main Home button, you are automatically returned to this page when you reopen the book.

Jump to a specific page

When you're reading a book, you often want to go to a specific page. Here's how:

1. **Tap anywhere near the center of the page you're reading to summon page navigator controls, if they're not already visible.**

   The controls are labeled in Figure 5-10.

2. **Drag your finger along the slider at the bottom of the screen until the chapter and page number you want appear.**

3. **Release your finger and *voilà* — that's where you are in the book.**

Go to table of contents

Books you read on your iPad have tables of contents, just like almost any other book. Here's how you use a table of contents on your iPad:

1. **With a book open on your iPad, tap the Table of Contents/Bookmark button near the top of the screen.**

   The Table of Contents screen shown in Figure 5-11 appears.

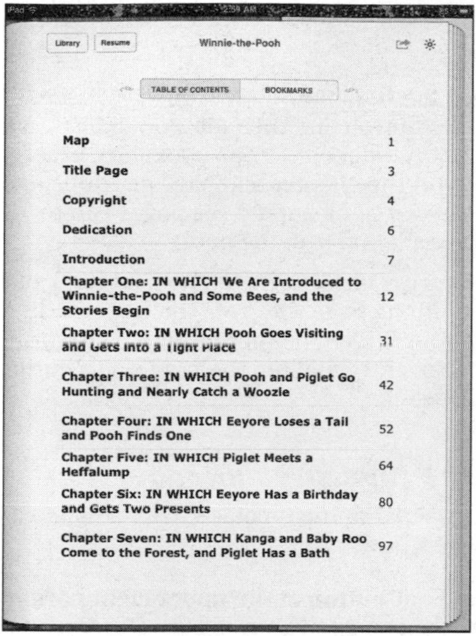

Figure 5-11: The table of contents for *Winnie-the-Pooh*.

2. **Tap the chapter, title page, or another entry to jump to that page.**

   Alternatively, tap the Resume button that appears at the top left of the screen to return to the previous location in the book.

Add bookmarks

Occasionally, you want to bookmark a specific page so that you can easily return to it. To insert a bookmark on a page, display the navigation tools and tap the Bookmark icon at the top right. A fancy-looking red ribbon appears, indicating that you've bookmarked the page.

After you set a bookmark, here's what you can do with it:

- ✔ **To find the bookmark later,** tap the Table of Contents button and then tap Bookmarks (if it's not already selected). Your bookmark is listed along with the chapter and page citations and the date you bookmarked the page. Tap to return to that page in the book.

- ✔ **To remove a bookmark,** tap the red bookmark ribbon on the page. Or, from the bookmarks list, swipe your finger in either direction along a bookmark entry and tap the red Delete button that appears.

Change the type size and font

If you want to enlarge the typeface size (or make it smaller), here's how:

1. **Tap the Font button at the upper-right corner of the screen (refer to Figure 5-10).**

2. **Tap the uppercase *A*.**

   The text swells up right before your eyes so that you can pick a size you're comfortable with. To make it smaller, tap the lowercase *a* instead.

If you want to change the fonts, tap the Fonts button and then tap the font style you want to switch to. The currently selected font style is indicated by a check mark.

Search inside and outside a book

If you want to find a passage in a book but just can't remember where it is, try searching for it. Here's how:

1. **Tap the magnifying glass Search icon to enter a search phrase on the virtual keyboard that slides up from the bottom.**

   All the occurrences in the book turn up in a window under the Search icon.

2. **Tap one of the items to jump to that portion of the book.**

You can also search Google or the Wikipedia online encyclopedia using the buttons at the bottom of the search results. If you do so, the iBooks app closes and the Safari browser fires up Google or Wikipedia, with your search term already entered. To return to the book, tap the iBooks icon again to reopen the app. You are returned to the page where you left off.

Perusing with Newsstand

With the success of iBooks, Apple decided to add a similar app to the iPad for reading magazine and newspaper subscriptions — and *Newsstand* was born. You notice the similarities immediately, since Newsstand uses the same "virtual shelf" navigation system as iBook. However, you don't use iBookstore to purchase your periodicals; you'll find a separate section of the App Store has been added just for this purpose.

To shop for a subscription, tap the Newsstand icon, then tap the Store icon. The App Store appears, already set to display periodical subscriptions. Like any other type of iPad app, you can search or browse the titles, or tap a subscription thumbnail to see additional information. When you've decided on a subscription, tap the price/Free button. Once the periodical is downloaded into Newsstand, simply tap the cover to begin reading.

Ah, but by definition, a periodical needs . . . well . . . periodic updating! That's where the fun begins within Newsstand: The app automatically downloads the new issues of your subscriptions, and indicates that new content has arrived by displaying an alert! (Look for the red circle that highlights how many new issues you have to read.)

Chapter 6

Gotta Love Those Apps!

. . . .

In This Chapter

▶ Browsing for cool apps

▶ Searching for specific apps

▶ Getting apps onto your iPad

▶ Managing iPad apps

▶ Social Media apps — even better on an iPad

. . . .

*O*ne of the best things about the iPad is that you can download and install apps created by third parties. At the time of this writing, more than 300,000 apps are available in the iTunes App Store. Many apps are free but others cost money. In this chapter, we take a broad look at apps you can use with your iPad. You discover how to find apps on your computer or your iPad, and you find some basics for managing your apps.

Tapping the Magic of Apps

Apps enable you to use your iPad as a game console, a streaming Netflix player, a recipe finder, a sketchbook, and much, much more. You can run three different categories of apps on your iPad:

✔ **Apps made exclusively for the iPad:** This is the newest kind, so you find fewer of these than the other two types. These apps won't run on an iPhone or iPod touch, so don't bother to try them on either device.

✔ **Apps made to work properly on an iPad, iPhone, or iPod touch:** This type of app can run on any of the three devices at full resolution. What is the full-screen resolution for each device? Glad you asked. For the iPhone and iPod touch, it's 320 x 480 pixels; for the iPad, it's 1024 x 768 pixels.

✔ **Apps made for the iPhone and iPod touch:** These apps run on your iPad but only at iPhone/iPod touch resolution (320 x 480) rather than the full resolution of your iPad (1024 x 768).

You can double the size of an iPhone/iPod touch app by tapping the little 2x button in the lower-right corner of the screen; to return it to its native size, tap the 1x button.

Frankly, most iPhone/iPod apps look pretty good at 2x size, but we've seen a few that have jagged graphics and don't look as nice. Still, with three hundred thousand or more to choose from, we're sure that you can find a few that make you happy.

Figure 6-1 shows you what this looks like.

You can obtain and install apps for your iPad in two ways:

✔ On your computer

✔ On your iPad

In the days before iCloud, if you downloaded an app on your computer, it wasn't available on your iPad until you synced the iPad with your computer — under iOS 5, however, apps that you download on your iPad or computer are automatically pushed to your other iOS devices via iCloud.

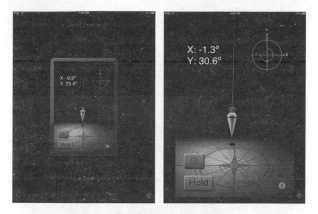

Figure 6-1: iPhone or iPod touch apps run at a smaller size (left) but can be "blown up" to double size (right).

To use the App Store on your iPad (or to sync wirelessly using iCloud), it must be connected to the Internet.

But before you can use the App Store on your iPad or your computer, you first need an iTunes Store account. If you don't already have one, we suggest that you launch iTunes on your computer, click Sign In near the upper-right corner of the iTunes window, and then click Create New Account and follow the on-screen instructions.

Using Your Computer to Find Apps

Okay, start by finding cool iPad apps using iTunes on your computer. Follow these steps:

1. **Launch iTunes.**
2. **Click the iTunes Store link in the sidebar on the left.**

3. **Click the App Store button at the top of the window.**

   The iTunes App Store appears, as shown in Figure 6-2.

App Store link   Search iTunes Store

iTunes Store (in sidebar)   iPad tab

Scroll bar

See All link

Figure 6-2: The iTunes App Store, in all its glory.

4. **(Optional) If you want to look only for apps designed to run at the full resolution of your iPad, click the iPad tab at the top of the window.**

Browsing the App Store from your computer

After you have the iTunes App Store on your screen, you have a couple of options for exploring its virtual

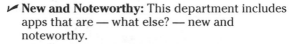

aisles. This section introduces the various "departments" available from the main screen.

The main departments are featured in the middle of the screen, and ancillary departments appear on either side of them, so some are not visible in Figure 6-2:

- ✔ **New and Noteworthy:** This department includes apps that are — what else? — new and noteworthy.

 Look to the right of the words *New and Noteworthy.* See the words *See All?* That's a link; if you click it, you see *all* apps in this department on a single screen. Or, you can click and drag the scroll bar to the right to see more icons.

- ✔ **What's Hot:** This department appears below New and Noteworthy and includes apps popular with other iPad users.

- ✔ **Staff Favorites:** This department appears below What's Hot.

 Apple has a habit of redecorating the iTunes Stores every so often, so allow us to apologize in advance if things aren't exactly as described here when you visit.

You also see display ads for featured apps between the New and Noteworthy department and the What's Hot department.

Three other departments appear to the right, under the Top Charts heading: Paid Apps, one of our favorite departments; Free Apps; and Top Grossing Apps. The number one app in each department displays both its icon and its name; the next nine apps show text links only.

Finally, the App Store link near the top of the screen is also a drop-down menu (as are most of the other department links to its left and right). If you click and hold on most of these department links, a menu with a list of the department's categories appears. For example, if you click and hold on the App Store link, you can choose specific categories such as Books, Entertainment, and others from the drop-down menu, allowing you to bypass the App Store home page and go directly to that category.

Using the Search field

Browsing the screen is helpful, but if you know exactly what you're looking for, we have good news: There's a faster way! Just type a word or phrase into the Search field in the upper-right corner of the main iTunes window, as shown in Figure 6-3, and then press Enter or Return to initiate the search.

Figure 6-3: I want to use my iPad as a flashlight, so I searched for the word *flashlight*.

The little triangle to the right of each item's price is another drop-down menu. This one lets you give this app to someone as a gift, add it to your wish list, send an e-mail to a friend with a link to it, copy the link to this product to the Clipboard so that you can paste it elsewhere, or share this item on Facebook or Twitter.

Getting more information about an app

To find out more about an application icon, a featured app, or a text link on any of the iTunes App Store screens, just click it. A detail screen like the one shown in Figure 6-4 appears.

Figure 6-4: The detail screen for SketchBook Pro, a nifty drawing and painting app for your iPad.

This screen should tell you most of what you need to know about the application, such as basic product information and a narrative description, what's new in this version, the language it's presented in, and the system requirements to run the app.

Downloading an app

This part is simple. When you find an application you want to try, just click its Free App or Buy App button. When you do so, you'll have to log on to your iTunes Store account, even if the app is free.

After you log on, the app begins downloading. When it's finished, it appears in the Apps section of your iTunes library, as shown in Figure 6-5.

Figure 6-5: Apps that you download appear in the Apps section of your iTunes library.

> With iCloud, downloading an app to your iTunes library on your computer will automatically push it to your iPad. However, if your hardware doesn't support iCloud, you have to sync your iPad before the application will be available on it.

Using Your iPad to Find Apps

Finding apps with your iPad is almost as easy as finding them by using iTunes. The only requirement is
that you have an Internet connection of some sort —
Wi-Fi or wireless data network — so that you can
access the iTunes App Store and browse, search,
download, and install apps.

Browsing the App Store on your iPad

 To get started, tap the App Store icon on your
iPad's Home screen. After you launch the App
Store, you see six icons at the bottom of the
screen, representing six ways to interact with
the store, as shown in Figure 6-6. The first four
icons at the bottom of the screen — Featured,
Genius, Top Charts, and Categories — offer
four ways to browse the virtual shelves of the
App Store. (The fifth and sixth icons we
cover a little later, in the section "Updating
and re-downloading an app.")

These icons are described as follows:

- ✔ **Featured:** Offers three tabs at the top of the
  screen: New (see Figure 6-6), What's Hot, and
  Release Date. These three tabs represent three
  different pages full of apps.

- ✔ **Genius:** Displays apps that you may like based
  on the apps that you've already installed.

- ✔ **Top Charts:** Offers lists of the Top Paid iPad
  apps and the Top Free iPad apps. These are, of
  course, the most popular apps that either cost
  money or don't.

Figure 6-6: The icons across the bottom represent the six sections of the App Store.

In the upper-left corner of the Top Charts screen is a Categories button. Tap it and you'll see a list of categories such as Books, Education, Games, Music, News, and Productivity, to name a few. Tap one of these categories to see the Top Paid and Top Free iPad apps for that category.

✔ **Categories:** Works a little differently: It has no tabs, and its main page contains no apps. Instead, it offers a list of categories such as Games, Entertainment, Utilities, Music, and Lifestyle, to name a few. Tap a category to see a page full of apps of that type.

Most pages in the App Store display more apps than can fit on the screen at once. A few tools help you navigate the multiple pages of apps:

✔ **The little triangles** at the top and bottom of the New and Noteworthy section are actually buttons you click to see the next or previous page of apps in that section. Tap them to see the next or previous page of apps.

✔ **The little dots** in the middle of the gray area above and below most sections (four dots appear in Figure 6-6) tell you how many pages the section contains; the white dot indicates which page you're currently viewing.

✔ Finally, tap **the See All link** at the top of most sections to (what else?) see all the apps in the section on the same screen.

Using the Search field

If you know exactly what you're looking for, rather than simply browsing, you can tap the Search field in the upper-right corner of the screen and type a word or phrase; then tap the Search key on the keyboard to initiate the search.

Finding details about an app

Now that you know how to find apps in the App Store, the following sections show you how to find out more about a particular application. After tapping an app icon as you browse the store or in a search result, you see a detail screen like the one shown in Figure 6-7.

 Remember that the application description on this screen was written by the developer and may be somewhat biased.

Figure 6-7: A typical detail screen for an iPad app.

The information you find on the detail screen on your iPad is similar to that in the iTunes screen you see on your computer. The links, rating, and requirements simply appear in slightly different places on your iPad screen. (See the section "Getting more information about an app," earlier in this chapter, for explanations of the main on-screen items.)

The reviews section differs most from the computer version. To read reviews from your iPad, scroll down to the bottom of any detail screen and you find a star rating for that application. At the bottom of that page is another link: More. Tap it to see (what else?) more reviews.

Downloading an app

To download an application to your iPad, follow these steps:

1. **Tap the price button near the top of its detail screen.**

   The gray price button is then replaced by a green rectangle that says Install App.

2. **Tap the Install App button.**

3. **When prompted, type your iTunes Store account password.**

   After you do, the App Store closes and you see the Home screen where the new application's icon will reside. The new app's icon is slightly dimmed and has the word *Loading* beneath it, with a blue progress bar near its bottom to indicate how much of the app remains to be downloaded.

4. **(Optional) If the app is rated 17+, click OK in the warning screen that appears after you type your password to confirm that you're over 17 before the app downloads.**

 iCloud comes to the rescue again! The application will automatically appear in your iTunes library on your Mac or PC — no old-fashioned syncing with a USB cable necessary!

Updating and re-downloading an app

As mentioned earlier in this chapter, every so often the developer of an iPad application releases an update. If an update awaits you, a little number in a circle appears on the Updates icon at the bottom of the screen. Follow these steps to update your apps:

1. **Tap the Updates icon if any of your apps needs updating.**

If you tap the Updates button and see (in the middle of the screen) a message that says All Apps are Up-to-Date, none of the apps on your iPad requires an update at this time. If apps need updating, they appear with Update buttons next to them.

2. **Tap the Update button that appears next to any app to update it.**

   If more than one application needs updating, you can update them all at once by tapping the Update All button in the upper-right corner of the screen.

 If you try to update an application purchased from any iTunes Store account except your own, you're prompted for that account's ID and password. If you can't provide them, you can't download the update.

After you've paid for an app, you can download it again if you need to, and you don't have to pay for it again. To re-download an app, open the App Store on your iPad and tap the Purchased icon at the bottom of the screen. The App Store displays all of the apps you've downloaded in the past — to make a specific app easier to find, use the Search box in the upper right corner of the screen, or tap the Sort By field to display apps sorted by Most Recent or App Name.

If an app is currently installed, it bears the Installed label. You can re-download an app that you deleted by tapping the iCloud icon next to the app name — the App Store prompts you for your Apple ID.

Working with Apps

Most of what you need to know about apps involves simply installing third-party apps on your iPad.

However, you might find it helpful to know how to delete, review, or report a problem with an app.

Deleting an app

You can delete an application in two ways: in iTunes on your computer or directly from your iPad.

To delete an application in iTunes, click Apps in the sidebar and then do one of the following:

- ✔ Click the app to select it and press the Backspace or Delete key on the keyboard.
- ✔ Click the app to select it and then choose Edit↩ Delete.
- ✔ Right-click the app and choose Delete.

After taking any of the actions in this list, you see a confirmation dialog box that asks whether you're sure you want to remove the selected application. Click the Remove button to remove the app from your iTunes library, as well as from any iPad that syncs with your iTunes library. (This is the best option because iTunes reclaims the space that the app was taking on your computer's hard drive.) Click Cancel to keep the app.

Here's how to delete an application on your iPad:

1. **Press and hold any icon until all the icons begin to "wiggle."**
2. **Tap the little *x* in the upper-left corner of the application that you want to delete.**

   A dialog box appears, informing you that deleting this application also deletes all its data.
3. **Tap the Delete button.**

To stop the icons from wiggling, just press the Home or Sleep/Wake button.

Deleting an app from your iPad this way doesn't get rid of it permanently. It remains in your iTunes library (and takes up space on your computer's hard drive) until you delete it from iTunes, as described earlier in this chapter. Put another way: Even though you deleted the application from your iPad, it's still in your iTunes library. If you want to get rid of an application for good after you delete it on your iPad, you must also delete it from your iTunes library.

You also make icons wiggle to move them around on the screen or move them from page to page. To rearrange wiggling icons, press and drag them one at a time. If you drag an icon to the left or right edge of the screen, it moves to the next or previous Home screen. You can also drag two additional icons to the dock (where Safari, Mail, Photos, and Music live) and have a total of six apps available from every Home screen.

Socializing with Social Media Apps

Your iPad doesn't include any specific social media apps right out of the box, but you can add free client apps for the major social media networks including Facebook, MySpace, Twitter, and the new kid on the block, Apple's Game Center.

iOS 5 also has support for Twitter built into many of the Apple iPad apps — you can tweet directly from Safari, Photos, Camera, YouTube and Maps. Things get even better: You only need to enter your Twitter username and password one time (on the Twitter pane within Settings), and your iPad signs you in automatically ever after! You can choose to add your location to your tweets, too.

As of this writing, only Game Center and Twitter offer client apps that run natively on the iPad. While we are certain they'll get around to releasing bigger, better, iPad-friendly apps soon, for now all we can show you are the iPhone versions of their apps running at iPhone resolution.

Note that you don't necessarily need an app to participate in social networking. Three of the four networks we mentioned can be fully utilized using Safari on your iPad. And frankly, unlike the iPhone, where the Safari experience was hampered by the tiny screen and keyboard, all three Web sites are eminently usable on your iPad. So, if you want to check them out and don't feel like downloading their apps, here are their URLs:

- ✔ Facebook: www.facebook.com
- ✔ MySpace: www.myspace.com
- ✔ Twitter: http://twitter.com

Game Center

Game Center is the odd duck of the bunch. As we mentioned, unlike the others, there is no Game Center Web site; you have to use the Game Center app that came with your iPad. And unlike the others, which are broad-based and aimed at anyone and everyone, Game Center is designed for a specific segment of the iPad (and iPhone and iPad touch) universe, namely users who have one or more games on their iPads (or other devices).

Game Center acts as a match-up service, letting you challenge your friends or use Auto-Match to challenge a stranger who also happens to be looking for someone to play against. Figure 6-8 shows Bob about to initiate a two-player game of Flight Control HD.

Figure 6-8: Invite a stranger to play (Auto-Match) or click the Invite Friend button to challenge a friend.

Of course, to make a social network like Game Center a success, there needs to be lots of games that support Game Center. And therein lies the rub. Because Game Center is relatively new (born in late 2010), there are only a few dozen games available with Game Center support.

Although there may not be many Game Center-aware games yet, the ones that are available already include such top sellers as Angry Birds, Real Racing HD, Pinball HD, and the World Series of Poker.

Facebook

The Facebook iPhone app, shown in Figure 6-9, makes it easy to access the most popular Facebook features with a single finger tap.

Figure 6-9: A Facebook Live Feed as seen in the Facebook iPhone app.

That said, we hope the Facebook iPad app is something more than just a higher-resolution version of the iPhone app. Why? Well, the iPad, unlike the iPhone, has a thoroughly usable Web browser, and quite frankly, we'd rather look at our Facebook Live Feed in Safari than in the Facebook iPhone app.

On the other hand, Safari can't provide push notifications for Facebook events such as messages, wall posts, friend requests and confirmations, photo tags, events, and comments, whereas the iPhone app does all that and more.

The bottom line is that there's nothing to prevent having the best of both worlds. So if you're a heavy Facebook user, consider using the Facebook iPhone app for some things (like push notifications and status updates) and Safari for others (like reading your Wall or Live Feeds).

MySpace

The MySpace app provides us with the same dilemma as the Facebook app (and the official Twitter app, which we get to in a minute): As of this moment, an iPad version isn't available. And as far as we can see, you don't have any reason to use the iPhone app 'cause it doesn't even offer push notifications (as the Facebook app does).

Take a look at the MySpace app in Figure 6-10 so you can see what we mean.

Again, we reserve the right to say something nice about the MySpace iPad app if they introduce one. But for now we think you'll enjoy interacting with MySpace more if you use Safari.

Twitter

Twitter puts a slightly different spin on social networking. Unlike Facebook or MySpace, it doesn't try to be encompassing or offer dozens of features, hoping that some of them will appeal to you. Instead, Twitter does one thing and does it well. That thing is letting its users post short messages called *tweets* quickly and easily from a variety of platforms including Web browsers, mobile phones, smartphones, and other devices.

Figure 6-10: A MySpace home page as seen in the MySpace iPhone app.

Twitter users then have the option of "following" any other Twitter user's tweets. The result is a stream of short messages like the ones seen in Figure 6-11. As we mention earlier in the chapter, Apple has recognized Twitter's success by integrating support for tweeting in a number of iPad apps (the most obvious being Safari, Photos, and Maps).

Just how short are tweets? Glad you asked. You're limited to a mere 140 characters. That's barely longer than this Tip. So be as concise as possible.

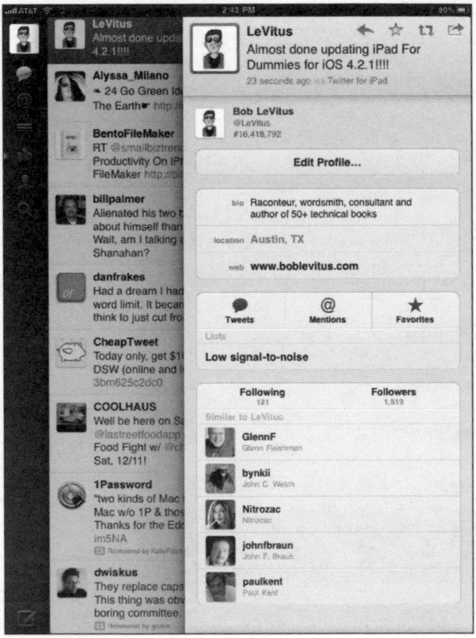

Figure 6-11: The official Twitter iPad app as seen through the eyes of Bob (@LeVitus).

Chapter 7

Ten Worthwhile Accessories

In This Chapter

▶ Covers

▶ Protective film

▶ Wireless keyboard

▶ Camera connector

▶ Digital AV adapter cable

▶ Spare charger

▶ Earphones, headphones, and headsets

▶ Speakers

▶ Extender cable

▶ iPad stand

Apple and several other companies are all too happy to outfit your iPad with extra doodads, from wireless keyboards and stands to battery chargers and carrying cases.

One thing is certain: If you see a "Made for iPad" label on the package, the developer is certifying that an electronic accessory has been designed to connect specifically to the iPad and meets performance standards established by Apple.

We start this accessories chapter with the options that carry Apple's own logo and conclude with worthwhile extras from other companies.

Casing the iPad

Apple's entry in this category, the Smart Cover, isn't technically a full case — it only covers the front of your iPad 2. However, the lightweight $39 Smart Cover has specially-designed magnets that align and hold it to the front of your iPad. When you remove the Smart Cover, your iPad wakes up automatically, and it goes to sleep automatically when you replace the Smart Cover. Finally, the versatile Smart Cover folds into two stands: one that makes typing on the virtual keyboard much easier, and one that acts as an easel for watching movies or displaying photos. At $39 for the polyurethane model and $69 for the leather model, the Smart Cover is superbly-designed minimalism.

If the Apple Smart Cover isn't quite what you're looking for, here are some other vendors of iPad 2 cases:

- **Abas** (www.abas.net).

- **Targus** (www.targus.com).

- **Griffin Technology** (www.griffintechnology.com).

- **iLuv** (www.i-luv.com).

- **Hard Candy Cases** (www.hardcandycases.com)

If you decide on a third-party case, verify first that you can use Apple cables and devices without having to remove the iPad from the case. Let's face it: slipping your iPad out of a case over and over is the definition of *hassle*.

Protecting the Screen

If you prefer not to use a case with your iPad, you might want to consider protective film for the iPad screen or even the whole device. We've tried these products on our iPhones in the past and have found them to perform as promised. If you apply them properly, they're nearly invisible and protect your iPad from scratches and scrapes without adding any bulk. Manufacturers of film protectors include Zagg (www.zagg.com), BodyGuardz (www.bodyguardz.com), and Best Skins Ever (www.bestskinsever.com).

Exploring Physical Keyboards

We think the various virtual keyboards that pop up just as you need them on the iPad are perfectly fine for shorter typing tasks, whether it's composing e-mails or tapping out a few notes. For most longer assignments, however, we writers are more comfortable pounding away on a real-deal physical keyboard. Fortunately, a physical keyboard for the iPad is an easy addition. Apple sells a wireless keyboard for a mere $69.

The Apple Wireless Keyboard is a way to use a top-notch aluminum physical keyboard without having to tether it to the iPad. It operates from up to 30 feet away from the iPad via wireless Bluetooth technology.

The Bluetooth keyboard takes two AA batteries. It's smart about power management too; it powers itself down when you stop using it to avoid draining those batteries. It wakes up when you start typing.

If you use a backpack, briefcase, messenger bag, or even a large purse, there's almost certainly room for the Apple Wireless Keyboard.

Connecting a Camera

The iPad delivers a marvelous photo viewer. If you take a lot of pictures, Apple's $29 iPad Camera Connection Kit is worth considering. It consists of the two components shown in Figure 7-1, either of which plugs into the 30-pin connector at the bottom of the iPad. One sports a USB interface that you can use with the USB cable that came with your camera to download pix. The other is an SD Card Reader that lets you insert the memory card that stores your pictures.

Figure 7-1: You have two ways to import images using the iPad Camera Connection Kit.

Connecting to a TV or Projector

The iPad has a pretty big screen for what it is, a tablet computer. But that display is still not nearly as large as a living room TV or a monitor you might see in a conference room or auditorium.

Projecting what's on the iPad's 1024 x 768 screen to a larger display is the very reason behind the iPad

Digital AV Adapter cable that Apple is selling for $39.
You can use it to connect your iPad to TVs, projec-
tors, and HDMI-capable (High-Definition Multimedia
Interface) displays. What for? To watch videos, slideshows, and presentations on the big screen.

 This HDMI connection provides 1080p HD resolution for apps and presentations and up to
720p for movies.

 If you'd like to dispense with the cables alto-
gether, iOS 5 introduces video mirroring
through AirPlay, allowing you to wirelessly display what you see on your iPad to a TV, projector, or HDMI display. There's one catch: that TV
or display device has to be connected to an
Apple TV that supports AirPlay.

Keeping a Spare Charger

With roughly 10 hours of battery life, a single charge
can more than get you through a typical work day with
your iPad. But why chance it? Having a spare charger
at the office can spare you from having to commute
with one. The Apple iPad 10W USB Power Adapter goes
for $29 and includes a lengthy 6-foot cord.

Listening the Wired and
Bluetooth Ways

You've surely noticed that your iPad does not come
with earphones or a headset. Apple offers the standard iPod earphones (with remote) separately for the
iPad at a reasonable $29. Alternatively, search
Amazon.com for headphones, earphones, or headsets, and you'll find thousands of each at prices rang-
ing from around $10 to over $1,000. Or, if you prefer

to shop in a brick-and-mortar store, Target, Best Buy, and the Apple Store all have decent selections, with prices starting at less than $20.

For earphones and earphone-style headsets, consider the Image S4 Headphones and S4i In-Ear Headset with Mic and 3-Button Remote, both from Klipsch. At around $79 and $99, respectively, they sound better than many similarly priced products and better than many more expensive offerings.

The idea behind Bluetooth stereo headphones, ear-phones, and headsets is simple: you can listen to music wirelessly up to 33 feet away from your iPad. If this sounds good to you, we suggest that you look for reviews of such products on the Web before you decide which one to buy. A good place to start is Amazon.com where we found over 300 stereo Bluetooth headsets, with prices starting as low as $15.

Listening with Speakers

You can connect just about any speakers to your iPad, but if you want decent sound, we suggest you look only at *powered* speakers and not *passive* (unpowered) ones. The difference is that powered speakers contain their own amplification circuitry and can deliver much better (and louder) sound than unpowered speakers.

Prices range from well under $100 to hundreds (or even thousands) of dollars. Most speaker systems designed for use with your computer, iPod, or iPhone work well as long as they have an Aux input or a dock connector that can accommodate your iPad.

Docking with an Extender Cable

Because of its much larger size compared to an iPod or iPhone, you can't just dock the iPad into a speaker system designed for the smaller devices. All is not lost if you're partial to those speakers and still want to connect the iPad. CableJive (cablejive.com) sells a dockXtender cable that lets you dock your iPad from a distance; it's described as a 30-pin Male to Female Extension cable. Versions come in black and white in two standard lengths: $25.95 for a 2-foot length and $31.95 for 6 feet.

Keeping Your iPad Upright

The Griffin A-Frame ($49.99) is so unusual we just had to include it. As you can see in Figure 7-2, it's a dual-purpose desktop stand made of heavy-duty aluminum. You can open it to hold your iPad in either portrait or landscape mode for video watching, displaying pictures, or reading. In this upright mode, it's also the perfect companion for the Apple Wireless Keyboard or any other Bluetooth keyboard. Or, close the legs and lay it down, and it puts your iPad at the perfect angle for using the on-screen keyboard.

Photos courtesy of Griffin Technology

Figure 7-2: The Griffin A-Frame is a unique, dual-purpose tabletop stand for your iPad.

Soft silicone padding keeps your iPad from getting scratched or sliding around, and the bottom lip is designed to accommodate the charging cable in portrait mode. Furthermore, it works with many third-party cases, including Griffin's flexible and hard-shell cases, among others.